Winning My Way

BY JIM DONNAN
with Lou Sahadi

*The Glory Years
of Marshall Football*

─────── *Foreword by* ───────
Bill Parcells & Barry Switzer

ACKNOWLEDGMENTS

To Kemmeth Rivers, whose dedicated efforts under an excruciating deadline helped make this book possible; special thanks also to Michelle Porter, Gary Richter, Linda Giles, Edna Justice and Tammy Donnan.

Published by Tiger Press
            P.O. Box 42
            Palisades, NY 10964
Printing by Chapman Printing Co.

Designed by Kemmeth R. Rivers
Cover photo by Sharron Swann
Inside photography by Rick Haye, Marilyn Testerman-Haye, Sharron Swann, Jim Gargus, Mike Kirtner and John Montanez. Additional photos from the Donnan family photo albums.

ISBN 0-9642530-0-3

Printed in the United States of America

TABLE OF CONTENTS

DEDICATIONS

For my dad...there have been millions of dads, but James M. Donnan, Jr. was the best.

- Jim Donnan

To long suffering Thundering Herd fans who waited a lifetime for Marshall football glory, and to Ernie Salvatore who somehow survived writing about all those desolate years.

- Lou Sahadi

FOREWARD

Jim and I met in Florida in 1972, while we were coaching together at Florida State. During the next twenty-two years, we developed a friendship between ourselves and our families.

We have kept in close contact and Jim has talked with me about every coaching move he has ever made. I assured him when he went to Marshall that there was great potential for Marshall to become a championship program.

Obviously, he has exhibited the characteristics that have always made him a successful coach in some major programs. He is very close to the players and is one of the most competitive people I have ever known.

Even though we don't get to see each other as much as we used to, we still keep in touch. He is one of the outstanding coaches in the country and I sincerely enjoy our friendship.

BILL PARCELLS
Head Coach
New England Patriots

Without question, Jim Donnan is one of the finest offensive coaches I was ever associated with in college football.

During the last four years I coached at Oklahoma with Jim as my offensive coordinator, we won three Big Eight Conference Championships and one National Championship while compiling a 42-6 record. His offenses were the best in the nation in rushing and scoring.

BARRY SWITZER
Head Coach
Dallas Cowboys

GROWING UP
IN NORTH CAROLINA

The first thing that caught my eye when Lee Moon was driving me around Huntington in the spring of 1990 was the fire hydrants that were painted green and white. I hadn't seen anything like that before and it struck me a bit odd. When I was a kid growing up in Rock Hill, South Carolina, the hydrants around town were painted red. I thought all fire hydrants were that color like in the comic books. It brought back a flood of memories from my youth.

I was an only child and had a happy childhood as long as I was participating in sports. My earliest recollection of childhood was when I was two years old. I was playing in the backyard of our little house and I remember seeing the telephone repairmen climbing up the big poles. I thought to myself, that seems like fun. Some kids that age go for marbles or maybe a red truck. I decided to go for the pole. Before my mother realized it, I climbed to the very top. Unfortunately, I had no idea how to get down.

My mother did. When she came out of the house to check on me and saw me on top of the pole, she didn't panic.

"Jimmy, don't move," she warned. "I'm going into the house for just a minute and I'll be right back."

She did come right back and about five minutes later a big fire truck pulled up next to the pole. A couple of firemen braced a ladder against the pole and one of them climbed up and got me. My mother didn't scold me. She just kept shaking her head.

"Jimmy, how in heaven's name did you ever climb that pole?" she asked.

I just shrugged my shoulders. Looking back, I guess at that early age I had an innate desire to compete. I saw a telephone man climb a pole and my natural instincts took over. I wanted to do the same thing the phone man had done. It became a pattern I developed as a child, wanting to compete at anything that appeared as a challenge to me. Quite naturally, sports offered the most challenges and as I grew older I started going to the YMCA every day and competed against bigger kids at any activity that interested me. I was only six when I lined up to play in a Ping-Pong tournament. One of the bigger kids came over and said I was too small to play, even though the kid in front of me didn't object. That bothered me.

That evening I went home and waited to talk to my father. He was a banker, an officer at the Wachovia Bank. He had been a good athlete before he left for the Army and I guess that's where my love for athletics came from. As I grew up, he was my hero. He was always there for me and was everything one expected in a father, even-tempered, consistent and disciplined with a strong set of values. As soon as he walked through the door, I approached him.

"Dad, I need to talk to you."

"What's wrong, son?" he asked.

"Nothing's really wrong, sir."

"Then what's the problem?"

"It's just that I would like for you to buy me a Ping-Pong table."

"Now, what would a six-year-old want with a Ping-Pong table? You're a bit young for that, son."

"Well, it's just that they wouldn't let me play in the tournament down at the Y."

"Why not?"

"Ah, they said I was too small. But Dad, I know I can do it. Honest."

I got my Ping-Pong table and played with the kids in the neighborhood every chance I got. My mother saw how determined I was to excel. Although my mom was kind of a mother hen and worried about everything, she worked hard to provide me with guidance. She wanted me to be successful in whatever I did, and at six years of age I wanted to be the best Ping-Pong player in town. In many ways, I received a great amount of inspiration from her. She drilled into me the importance of being the best that I could be. She always told me, "Never accept anything but the best you can be." I have never forgotten that.

Playing Ping-Pong was my first organized competition. Remembering Mom's words, I wanted to be the best player not only in town, but also in the state. I went on to win the state championship in every division I entered, 10 and under, 12 and under, 14 and under, 16 and under, and all the way up to 18 and under. Then, just like that, I stopped playing. I had accomplished what I set out to do. There is no doubt in my mind that Ping-Pong initiated my desire not only to compete, but to win.

When I was in the third grade, Dad was transferred to the bank in Asheville, North Carolina. It was the first of several moves our family made while I was small. The first place I headed was to the Y. It was a lot bigger than the one in Rock Hill. I made friends quickly, but I talked about Rock Hill so much some of the kids actually thought that was my name. One summer the Y had a leadership conference at Black Mountain, North Carolina, and I had the chance to attend. I was nine years old and I had my first opportunity to see coaches and athletes assembled in great numbers under one roof. It made quite an impression on me. I came away with a strong feeling of what it took to become a successful athlete and I was determined to become one. I know one thing; being able to play with bigger kids helped me to achieve my goals much quicker.

I played a lot of sports as a kid. Sports were my only hobby. My favorite was basketball, believe it or not. If the three-point basket had been in effect when I was growing up, I might have stayed with basketball. I wasn't very big, but I could pop 'em pretty good from outside. One of my funniest experiences came in a basketball tournament after we had moved to Burlington, North Carolina. We were playing in an all-star tournament in Greenville, South Carolina, when I was in the sixth grade. One of the kids on the other team showed up to play with peroxided hair. He stood out like a rooster in a hen house, but the guys on our team thought it was cool. After practice we all got together and decided to do the same thing. Now we had 12 kids with the same hair. We were a little worried about what the coach would say to us, but we figured we were all in it together and it was a team effort, so how mad could he be? He didn't say a word. He just took one look at us in the locker room, shook his head and walked away.

By living in Burlington, I was right in the middle of Raleigh, Durham, Chapel Hill, Winston-Salem and Atlantic Coast Conference country. If you were really into sports it was heaven. I grew up going to Duke, Carolina, Wake Forest and State games and watching guys like Billy Packer and Art Heyman. When I was in the seventh grade I had the chance to attend Frank McGuire's basketball camp after Carolina won the 1957 championship. McGuire was New York all the way, with a strong presence about him. He was dapper, with his wavy hair, and always seemed to be in control. He was popular in New York, enjoying years of success with St. John's. Even though he was strictly big city, he made a decision to leave the bright lights for Chapel Hill. His son was physically impaired and he felt it would be better for him to grow up away from the hustle and bustle of New York. That told me a great deal about the man.

McGuire had his championship team at the camp. Seeing and participating with all those champion players was one of the biggest thrills I had as a kid. Another thrill was watching my sports hero Mickey Mantle play. I loved the Yankees and my dad took me to Charlotte, North Carolina, one spring day to watch the Yankees play an exhibition game on their way to New York. Mickey didn't hit one that day but Johnny Mize did. He hit one so far it's probably still going down river. I was impressed that a big guy like Mize could swing so easily and hit a ball so far. It was just awesome to a ten-year-old.

We had some good athletes of our own in Burlington. No one was of superstar magnitude. It's just that we stuck together. In my last year at Williams High School we had one of the best football teams in the school's history. Nine of us received football scholarships. I played single wing tailback and had offers from a half dozen schools but narrowed it down to three: North Carolina State, North Carolina and Clemson. My mother was hoping I'd pick Davidson for the academics. I was too much into football, though.

It wasn't hard for me to pick State. My football hero was Roman Gabriel and he had a great career at State, even though the teams he played on weren't that good. I really admired the way he threw a football. He had great arm strength and I was convinced he could have thrown the ball the length of the field. He was all I wanted to be as a quarterback. I remember sitting in the stands and thinking, if I could throw a ball half as good as Roman, I'd be happy.

When I attended college, freshmen couldn't play on the varsity team. The three-year rule was in effect back in 1963. Instead, I played on the freshmen team and was the starting quarterback. I was starting to feel pretty good about myself. It's funny how life can be at times. Gene Hamilton, the kid in Asheville who wanted to play Ping-Pong with me at the Y that day, got me turned on to tennis. I had never played tennis before, preferring baseball, but his father, Jim, taught me so Gene would have someone to play. Well, as things turned out I played No. 1 at State and Gene was No. 1 at North Carolina.

Playing tennis ended my baseball career. During my freshman year in high school I had to make a decision to play baseball or tennis after the football and basketball seasons ended. I liked both sports, although tennis was relatively new to me. I had been playing baseball since Little League and by now I was a good hitter. I had a reputation of busting 'em over the fence. I decided to ask my father for advice. As always, he was there for me and I valued his opinion.

"Dad, I need some help making a decision about tennis and baseball."

"In what regard?" he asked.

"I don't know which one to give up."

"Which one do you like the most?"

"That's the hard part. I like both but I can play only one in the summer."

"Well, then, the way I see it you're better off with tennis because it can carry over."

He was right. As much as I participated in team sports, it is the one-on-one challenge that creates a tough competitor. Tennis is like that. Ping-Pong is too for that matter. I can recall even participating in a yo-yo contest and being competitive. I was only twelve years old when McDonald's opened its first restaurant in Burlington and they sponsored a yo-yo tournament. I won the contest and the $50 prize. Later that year the representatives of Duncan Yo-Yo Company came by my grade school and sponsored a contest. The prize was a sweater with Duncan Yo-Yo written across the front. I won that, too. It all boils down to that one word, competitiveness. I relish the challenge and the victory.

Football was no different. I was redshirted during my sophomore year at State in 1964, which was no big deal. All the colleges used that method to preserve an athlete's eligibility if they had several athletes at one position. However, being red-shirted meant that I wouldn't get to play with my best friend Bill Gentry. He was a tight end and a good one and we would always talk about how I would throw him the winning touchdown pass with the clock ticking down as he went into the end zone. Before the 1967 season, Bill suffered a cerebral hemorrhage. He has come back a long way since then, but it's been difficult on him all these years. That one unfortunate incident in which Bill almost died taught me that, indeed, there is life after football.

Sitting out a year was very beneficial to me. In high school I played under a single wing system. However, I was a better passer than a runner. At State, coach Earl Edwards emphasized a multiple offense, and the year I worked out with the varsity enabled me to understand the rudiments of the system. Besides, Edwards went into the season with three quarterbacks who were close in ability and it wouldn't have helped one bit if I was activated.

I enjoyed running plays against the varsity at practice every day. Each week I was implementing the opposing team's offense. One week I was Joe Namath. Another week I was Steve Spurrier. Who had it better than me? I didn't know it then but it served as a foundation for coaching. Instead of learning and playing one system, I was now exposed to four or five. The versatility enabled me to expand my knowledge of football.

I was the back-up quarterback my sophomore year and didn't get to play too much. However, by the time I was a junior, I was the starter. We opened the 1966 season at Michigan State, a powerhouse. They had a strong defense led by end Bubba Smith and linebacker George Webster, both of whom were All-Americans. They went on to great professional careers, Smith with the Baltimore Colts and Webster with the Houston Oilers. Bubba got me on a sack one time and really hit me hard. I got up aching.

"You just got hit by an All-American," remarked Smith. "Now you know what an All-American hit feels like. You'll fear me every time you try to pass."

I glared straight at him.

"I'll be here," I snapped.

We finished the season 5-5 but did well in the ACC, going 5-2. I learned a lot of football my junior year. Those ten games felt like a hundred but there was still more to learn. I made a vow to myself before my senior season that I wanted to make something happen, to be part of something big. It almost happened, too. I'll always remember my final season because we came within a foot of becoming national champions and wouldn't that have been something, the something I was looking for to happen.

The dream of an unbeaten season was becoming a reality late that autumn. We were 8-0 and focused and we had already clinched a bowl bid. We had two games left and if we won both of them, then we could begin thinking about becoming national champions along with UCLA and Southern Cal, who were also unbeaten. Both of the remaining games were on the road, the first at Penn State and the other at Clemson, both extremely difficult places to play. Penn State known as Happy Valley with its 85,000 fans, and Clemson known as Death Valley with its 80,000 fans. I didn't look forward to being at either place.

The Penn State game was the killer. We were putting our perfect season on the line against Penn State and its rookie coach, Joe Paterno. The game went to the wire. In the final minutes of the game, we were losing, 13-6, when we pieced together a drive to the Penn State goal line. On fourth down and goal, I was facing the biggest play I had ever called in my life.

My adrenaline was flowing. I was pumped as we broke the huddle, and I planted my feet under the center, waiting for the snap. On a quick count, I cleanly handed the ball to our fullback. Less than a measly yard and we would be looking at 9-0, or at worse, 8-0-1. It appeared as if the entire Penn State team keyed on our fullback. As soon as he tucked in my handoff, he was buried. I couldn't believe they stopped him short of going over the goal line. I couldn't think. I was numb. I was looking for a penalty, anything that would have given us another chance.

One of our defensive players had to jar me back to reality, to get me off the field. I still couldn't believe they had stopped us. I wanted to run the play over and carry the ball myself. We were so close. I stood on the sidelines and didn't remember the remaining seconds of the game. My head was spinning. Everything was a blur. It wasn't until later that I learned that Penn State took a safety rather than risk losing the ball on a fumble, making the final score 13-8. It was a long ride back to Raleigh. I don't remember anyone saying a word. How could we? The unbeaten dream, one that might have turned into a national championship, was gone. It became even a longer night when I found out that both UCLA and Southern Cal had lost. We could have been No. 1 that night, an honor that had never happened in the history of N.C. State football.

We were still emotionally drained when we went to play Clemson a week later. I could tell all week at practice that we had lost our pop. I tried to talk it up among the players, but I guess I didn't do a good job. At 8-1, I suppose we shouldn't have been down. After all, we were having the best year in State football history. But we all knew we had come so close to a possible national championship only to see it slip away. Clemson was waiting for us, especially their defense. They shut us down and beat us, 14-6. I wasn't exactly happy the way our offense was going, although I must admit both Penn State and Clemson played exceptional defense.

Despite the two straight defeats, our season wasn't a complete loss. We got an invitation to play the University of Georgia in the Liberty Bowl in Memphis. Vince Dooley was beginning to establish his legend as the best coach in Georgia's history. One of his assistants was Erik Russell, who later coached Georgia Southern and walloped Marshall 63-31 in 1989, the year before I became head coach. It was another of life's ironies that so often happens in sports. Georgia was a member of the Southeastern Conference, which carried a bigger reputation than the ACC. Beating them would be meaningful both from State's standpoint and also from the Conference's. We got focused enough to win, 14-7, and finish 9-2, the best record in State's history. I was voted the MVP of the game and later the ACC Player of the Year. But the one thing that made my mom proudest was that for the second straight year I was on the ACC's all-academic team.

Mom never stopped saying, "I told you so." She was entitled.

COACHING
DAYS

I had a decision to make. My major brought up an interesting situation. Do I want to go into the private sector and work for one of the large mills like Burlington Industries back home in Burlington or remain in athletics? Before graduation, I had a private talk with Coach Edwards. I liked him. Not only was he a good coach, but he was also a good person. He had his players' interests at heart because he kept reminding us about the importance of education and the necessity of earning a degree. His words were nearly as effective as Mom's.

"Coach," I began, "I'm faced with a decision. It's not a football decision but a career one in that I don't know which direction to go, coaching or business."

"How much do you like football, son?" he asked.

"I like football a great deal, but it's my future that I'm concerned with here."

"I've observed you pretty closely ever since you redshirted that first season. Jim, I think you have the makings of being an excellent coach one day if you're willing to pay the price. You're intelligent, you're dedicated and you have a love for the game."

"But where or how do I start becoming a coach?"

"You can start right here, with me."

"Doing what?"

"For one thing, you can coach the freshman team. Then you can always help out with the quarterbacks on the varsity. That's a pretty good start right there."

"It sounds good, and deep down I guess I really belong in athletics."

"Look at it this way. If you realize after a year that you don't like coaching, then you can always turn to the business world. It's a progressive step in that if you go to business first and try to come back to coaching, it's much more difficult. You're young, son, you have your whole life ahead of you. A year won't matter."

The last remark sold me. Since I had played freshman football, I felt confident enough to know what was expected from the players and, at the same time, what was expected from the coaches. I left Coach Edwards' office chuckling to myself, remembering the first few weeks of freshman football and the adjustments I had been expected to make, not only in learning a new system but in getting along with other players from all around the country. I never had been out of the South so anybody north of the Mason-Dixon line was practically a foreigner to me.

This was my first experience dealing with players from up North. We had to find a way to play together, or for that matter, communicate with one another. We had quite a mix. I was the quarterback, we had a guy from Brooklyn at fullback, one from New Jersey at tailback and another one from Pittsburgh. We just weren't clicking the way we should. Finally, one day at practice, the kid from Brooklyn broke the tension.

"Do you always talk that slow?" he asked.

"I can talk even slower if you want me to."

Everybody laughed and from that moment we didn't have any more trouble communicating or clicking together as a team. I wanted to carry that over into coaching later in the summer when the freshmen from all over the country reported. Until then, I hung around the football offices every moment I could. I had graduated in January and so I had the entire spring to myself. I was fortunate. Al Michaels, our defensive coordinator, reached out to help me. He insisted that I should spend most of my time with him. He pointed out that I knew enough about the offense but that I needed to learn about the other side of the ball. "Defense and scouting is where learning to coach is happening," said Michaels. It made me think. How could I begin to coach, even at the freshman level, if I didn't know about defense? That spring, if anyone wanted me, they would have to call Coach Michaels' office.

I was the head freshman coach for two years. I also found out what coaches do in the off-season. I learned to become a fund raiser for the Wolfpack Club, which is the same as the Big Green at Marshall. Before I began my third year at State, things were starting to happen. I received a coaching offer from Florida State. It was time to talk to Edwards again.

"What do you think, coach?"

"Well, it's flattering to you, I know, and it's part of the business. That's not the only offer you'll ever receive. Assistant coaches bounce around from year to year."

"Should I take the offer, then?"

"I didn't necessarily mean that. I feel you belong at State, that your future is here. I've been pleased with what you have accomplished. But it's your decision. Selfishly, I would prefer that you stay here."

"Let me sleep on it. I want to talk it over with my wife."

I had known Mary Wright since junior high in Burlington. We had been married for five years now and whatever decision I made would affect her and our two little daughters, Tammy and Paige. When I went to bed that night, I felt it was better at this point to remain at State. I felt a sense of loyalty in that they gave me an opportunity to coach. I don't know how I would have started in the profession without Coach Edwards. Another reason that made me stay was the transition of the first black athletes in the school's history. I recruited Willie Burden and Charlie Young, both of whom went on to play pro ball. Charlie played for the Cowboys and Willie is now the athletic director at North Carolina A&T.

Although assistant coaches come and go as Edwards had me believe, I never expected him to leave the following summer. Not only was I shocked, because he never intimated that it was going to happen, but I was disappointed, too. I had remained at State out of loyalty to Edwards and now he was gone. I was ready to leave and would have if Michaels hadn't been named the head coach. He deserved it. The only trouble was, he was hired on an interim basis, just for a year until the football committee searched for a new head coach. Knowing all this, I still decided to stay. I owed it to Michaels. He had done a lot for me.

State hired Lou Holtz as the new head coach in 1972. Although he had excellent credentials, I was disappointed that Michaels wasn't retained. It was obvious that the athletic committee wanted to go in another direction with someone new. Holtz was highly successful at William & Mary and had earned a reputation as a great motivator. He offered to keep me on staff. I'm sure that he didn't particularly want me. He brought along his staff from William & Mary and was quite content with his assistant coaches. He was honest with me when I met him for the first time.

"Jim, the main reason I'm keeping you is that the athletic director told me to," admitted Holtz.

"I don't want to feel unwanted, that you are doing something you don't want to do," I said.

"Well, that's not exactly true. I need a liaison, somebody like you who knows the territory. You've done a good job here the last three years."

"What do you have in mind for me?"

"Look, I know the way Edwards did things and how you feel about Michaels. Just look at this as a new beginning. We're going to have some fun."

"How do I fit in?"

"Your main concern will be in the recruiting area. You will have to work your way up on my staff because the coaches I have are good and they've been with me a long time. But I'll give you some authority."

"I understand. I'll give it a shot and see how it works out."

Holtz was a bundle of energy. He was gung ho and very organized. I could see why he was a winner. He was very thorough and in the short time I was with him I learned a great deal about organization. He was in complete charge and I understood where he was coming from. But I wasn't happy and I wasn't involved with coaching as much as I would have liked. I decided it was time to leave. After a month, I told Holtz about my decision. He understood and wished me luck.

I had received an offer from North Carolina and another from Florida State. Since I had been in North Carolina all of my life, I felt I would be more comfortable in Chapel Hill. During the spring of 1974, I made the short drive from Raleigh. I kept thinking along the way, hey, I'm going to be coaching at North Carolina, which is State's biggest rival. Then I began to wonder, what am I getting myself into? As I got closer, I began to ask myself more questions. Will I be able to make the transition? After all, I had been at State for eight years and would be going into the enemy camp.

After three months, I still couldn't shake my years at State. I knew I couldn't stay at North Carolina even though Coach Bill Dooley had given me anything I needed. I called Coach Larry Jones at Florida State, not knowing whether he had filled the job he had offered me earlier. I felt I had nothing to lose and besides, I didn't know where else to turn. Although I didn't look forward to leaving my home state, I felt strongly that it was time I broke the link.

"Do you still have that opening?" I asked excitedly.

"As a matter of fact, yes," answered Jones. "We had a couple of applicants but we weren't that high on them."

"Are you still high on me?"

"Of course. What are you trying to tell me?"

"I'd like to come down and work for you."

"Isn't it working out at Carolina?"

"It's not that. Everybody has been great here. It's just that I have to break away from the area. I've been around here too long, all my life, and there is no question in my mind that I need a complete change of scenery. I need a whole new beginning, people, coaching environment, life-style, the whole nine yards. I never thought I'd ever say that."

"I understand completely. When can you get down here and get started?"

"I'll be there in a week. That sound okay?"

"You got it."

I was really looking forward to a totally new experience. Mary couldn't believe that we were actually leaving North Carolina. Tammy and Paige now had a baby brother, Todd, to help keep them busy. Kids being kids, we were certain they could find plenty to keep them happy in the Sunshine State.

I ended up hitting it off with Bill Parcells right away. I already felt the difference of coaching in another area of the country and I knew I was in for a new learning experience. I was in charge of the running backs and Parcells coached the linebackers. Off the field our families were close and we spent time together, never realizing that we would become lifelong friends. We played a great deal of tennis together. He had never played before but I taught him how and he became a good player. We also did a lot of talking, just two coaches with ideals and dreams. He was determined to become a head coach soon and he was ready. Bill was four years older and more ambitious than I was. He told me that when he became a head coach, he'd come after me.

Both of us were players' coaches. We related well with the kids but he was a bit tougher on them than I was. I knew he had the qualities of a head coach. He was perceptive and could really judge people well. He had a good feel for players as far as getting the best out of them and making them feel a part of the program. He carried all those virtues successfully to the National Football League. His achievement didn't surprise me, winning two Super Bowls with the New York Giants.

If there was anybody who liked tuna fish more than Bill I haven't met him. Without fail, Bill would eat a tuna fish sandwich every day. I don't recall ever seeing him without one at lunch time. We kidded him about it and called him Tuna. That's how he acquired the nickname and he carried it with him all through college and into the pros. Everybody thought he got the nickname because he was so big but it was really because of all those tuna fish sandwiches. He was the original "Charlie the Tuna."

I was at Florida State for only two years when I packed up the car again to return to North Carolina. Dooley offered me the job as chief recruiter for the university and also wanted me to coach the running backs. It was time to leave Tallahassee. Parcells had decided to do the same, the year before. Only he surprised me by going to Vanderbilt to work under Coach Steve Sloan.

When I returned to Chapel Hill for the 1974 season, I felt recharged. I thoroughly enjoyed the two years I spent at Florida State. I was exposed to a wide open style of football and we led the nation in passing one year. That broadened my coaching base immensely. I benefited from taking part in a totally new system. I had come a long way since single wing football in high school. Time does wonders. I didn't look at North Carolina as a rival any more, but as an opportunity. I had missed North Carolina in the two years I had been away. I guess I was still a country boy at heart but with a new perspective. I remembered what Parcells told me about being a head coach. I was ready to go forward with that in mind and North Carolina was as good a place as any to head in that direction. With five in the family now, I had to get my priorities in focus.

The first thing I learned about Dooley was he didn't like change. He was very much set in his ways and nobody could move him. There was no way I could introduce some of the wide open strategy I learned at Florida State. Nevertheless, his personality was consistent and he was easy to work for. Dooley had extremely well-organized practices and I made a note of that. However, he had an insatiable appetite for recruiting and he formulated it through a large staff. I didn't see how he could ever miss a high school prospect with all the bloodhounds he had searching the countryside. It was easy to see why he dominated recruiting in North Carolina and Virginia.

All too familiar was that I was reliving my years at North Carolina State. After I spent four years there, Earl Edwards left. Now it was happening again. After I put in four years at North Carolina, Dooley left to become the athletic director at Virginia Tech. Only this time, instead of going with him, I decided to hang in and apply for the vacant head coach job. I was only 30 years old, but after having been with three different programs, I felt I was ready. Dooley wished me luck, adding that he was disappointed that I wasn't going with him. I couldn't. If I was ever going to become a head coach, I felt his leaving would provide me with the best opportunity, despite my age.

Dooley had it made at North Carolina, but he was always in Dean Smith's shadow. Smith was becoming an icon with his successful basketball teams year after year. Even though we were beginning to dominate the ACC in football, Dooley realized he could never become the athletic director at Carolina like his brother, Vince, at Georgia and his best friend Johnny Majors, who was the assistant athletic director at Tennessee. The athletic director's job at Virginia Tech was worth a lot of money and was a good enough reason for Dooley to leave.

Although football and basketball coaches usually don't mix, I have tremendous respect for Dean. He is one of the most compassionate people I have ever known. He totally cares about people and he was always good to me. Besides his integrity and knowledge of basketball, I think it is his compassionate nature that contributes to his success.

There was an incoming freshman, Lawrence Taylor, that I wanted to coach. The first time I saw him on the field, he had star quality written all over him. He was smaller than in his days with the New York Giants, but he had a fierce look of determination in his eyes that set him apart from the other players. There was no doubt in my mind that he was a special athlete. However, I coached him only one year because I left North Carolina, disappointed at not getting the head coach's job that Dooley left open. I was told that I was looked upon as a Dooley man and the athletic board wanted to go in another direction. We had a good staff and Jim Dickey was later hired as head coach at Kansas State. Ironically, when I didn't get the Carolina job, it opened up the recruiting door for Danny Ford in North Carolina and he made the most of it.

It was time to load the wagon again. I had to move on.

chapter 3▶

OKLAHOMA YEARS

This time instead of going south, I was going west in 1978. Who was it that said, "Go west, young man, go west"? Horace Greeley was never a football coach but it was good enough for me and I followed his advice. Dickey offered me a position on his staff as an assistant coach in charge of quarterbacks and receivers which gave me more offensive responsibilities than I had had before. The money was good, too. Yet, I could have gone even further west. Parcells was now the head coach at the Air Force Academy and he kept a promise to me that he made when we were both at Florida State. As always, he was honest with me.

"Jim, I have a spot for you as I always said I would," began Bill.

"I was never worried about that," I interrupted.

"Let me finish. However, I don't think the job is right for you."

"Why not? I'll be coaching with you which is what I always looked forward to doing."

"I know, but this isn't quite right."

"Really."

"Yes, and here's why. It's good for me because I'm a head coach now but it's bad for you simply because there aren't many good players here and it's going to take a while to get them. It's not all that easy recruiting for a service academy and it will take some time to put together a winning team. As such, nobody will look at an assistant coach in a losing program."

"That makes a lot of sense, I guess."

As much as I wanted to coach with him again, he was right, although Kansas State didn't look much better. They had lost 20 games in a row and the program was far from promising. However, that very first season we managed to win four games, the biggest being against rival Kansas. After we beat them, we kept the scoreboard on for a week. Now, more than ever, Dickey knew of my desire to become a head coach and I always confided in him when I had an opportunity to interview.

The first time was at North Carolina State, of all places. But once again I was passed over when they picked Monte Kiffin. I felt certain that I would finally get my first head coaching job. It was all so natural. I had played at State and coached there for four years and was several years older now. The rejection convinced me that I would never get to coach State, which was what I always wanted. The following year I had a shot at the job at West Virginia University, but Don Nehlen beat me out. Ironically, if I had gotten that job, I never would have ended up at Marshall ten years later. Football, indeed, takes crazy bounces.

I remained at Kansas State for three years before driving my car for another ride, this time in the direction of the University of Missouri. I was beginning to think that I had made a mistake in my approach to becoming a head coach. Perhaps I would have been better off if I had begun at the I-AA level and then moved up to I-A. Then again I felt that it was just a case of bad luck. I was 35 now, so I was still young enough. While at Missouri, we beat Oklahoma twice, in 1981 and 1983. Oklahoma coach Barry Switzer didn't forget because when one of his assistants, Mack Brown, left in 1984, he offered me the job.

The Oklahoma years were the most rewarding coaching situation I had experienced. I was there five years, the most I had ever spent at any school, and who knows, I might still be there if Switzer had not left in 1989. No one impressed me more than Switzer. I had never been around anyone quite like him. He knew football. I couldn't believe his approach to the game. I'll never forget that first meeting.

"I've been coaching for twenty years and I'm not interested in coaching to some degree," he remarked.

That shocked me. He saw the look of astonishment on my face.

"But, I'll help you," he quickly added.

I let out a sigh. "In what way?"

"I want you to be in charge of the offense, to take complete charge of things."

"That's a lot of responsibility. I appreciate your confidence in me."

"If you have any problems, just come talk to me. My door is always open."

"You mean it's as simple as all that?"

"I believe in delegating authority and the offense is your responsibility."

He employed the same simple philosophy on defense. The defensive staff, under Gary Gibbs, did their thing, we did ours and Switzer did his. He was more into public relations and recruiting. Those were his strengths above all else. He was brilliant, a genius on offense. As much of a public figure as he was, he was also very loyal and private. The biggest difference I found with him and others I coached with was that Switzer didn't have an ego problem. He never worried about what people thought. He was always in the limelight but he never let it consume him.

Switzer was extremely good to me and was always there when I needed his input. He was truly a players' coach. He taught me a very important lesson; regardless of the situation, you play talent and not experience. That was strong. I also learned about being in the public eye. He was so visible and yet he knew how to react if things got carried away. I also learned another important lesson about coaching, namely how to be flexible and not worry about doing everything by the book. What I did and learned under Switzer during my five years at Oklahoma prepared me to be a head coach. Unquestionably, he has been the biggest influence in my career.

I regard my Oklahoma experiences as unique. Football was big in Oklahoma and we were expected to win and win big every year. It was as if we represented the entire state, and I say that without any disrespect to Oklahoma State University. My first three years in Norman we went 33-3, and when I left, we were 49-10. We won the national championship my very first year, in 1985, when we beat Penn State in the Orange Bowl. The other years, we were always in the hunt. I had changed an offense that was geared to the development of the passing game to one of a pure option game geared to the run.

By far, this was the best coaching situation I had experienced. The environment was perfect for football, winning football. Everyone in the state rallied around Oklahoma football. It was like a Saturday religion. Two of those three years, when we went 33-3, we led the nation in offense. Changing the offensive scheme was a smoother transition than I anticipated, made easier by the great athletes we had at Oklahoma. Troy Aikman was one. Keith Jackson was another and Brian Bosworth was still another one. Jamelle Holieway was also an exceptional athlete, taking over for Aikman when he was injured and was lost for a year.

One of the most difficult moments came when Aikman broke his leg during his sophomore season. We were so close to being the football team we wanted to be and suddenly we lost our top quarterback. Holieway stepped in and did an outstanding job in leading us to the national championship. That created a dilemma. Do we go back to the pass-option offense with Aikman or stick to the pure option with Holieway, who had demonstrated his athletic prowess?

I was torn between my feelings for Troy, and the realization it would be hard to bench Jamelle after he had led us to a national championship. Aikman had the best arm I had seen and Jamelle was a gifted runner who could also throw. I had several sleepless nights trying to reach a decision. Ultimately, it was Troy who made the decision for me. He believed he would be better off at another school since we had changed to the wishbone. I talked to Switzer about it.

"We have to stay with the wishbone," he said.

"It's hard not to, after the year we had," I remarked.

"We'll have to get him situated somewhere else. It'll be in his best interests."

"I hate to lose him. He'll definitely be a number one draft choice when he's through."

"I totally agree with you. That's why we have to make sure we get him into a program that'll utilize his abilities to the maximum."

"What do you have in mind?"

"Call three or four schools that can use someone like Troy and get their reactions."

The first call I made was to Terry Donohue at UCLA. He clearly indicated he was excited about having him transfer. Actually, Aikman was Donohue's number one recruiting prize in high school, but Troy wanted to stay in the Midwest, which was one reason why he chose Oklahoma. I also called Stanford, Miami and Arizona State. Everyone returned my calls except Stanford. I felt Stanford would be the perfect spot for Troy and I was puzzled why Jack Elway never called back. So, it boiled down to three schools and Troy decided on UCLA, much to Donohue's delight. Ironically, Jimmy Johnson, who had waited anxiously for Troy to pick Miami, later received his chance to coach him at Dallas where they won two Super Bowls together, in 1993 and 1994. Another crazy bounce of the football.

As good as Aikman was, he wasn't the best player I have ever coached. Keith Jackson, our tight end, simply dominated his position to be the best. He had such a talent for making the play when we needed it. All the great ones have that ability. He was a big play receiver - the type of receiver the pros love. But he was also a team player and accepted any role he was given. Not only was he talented, but he was also intelligent. He graduated in three-and-one-half years which says something about his intelligence and work ethic. Not many were aware of the sensitivity Jackson, as big and strong as he was, possessed. In his quiet moments, he loved playing the cello.

One year, when Jackson was only a sophomore, we put in a tight end reverse. Yes, he could run, too. I did have to sell Jackson on it before the Nebraska game, but he responded like the player he was. The first time we called the play, he ran 88 yards for a touchdown. Before the game, I had informed our radio play-by-play announcer John Brooks that we had put in the play so he wouldn't get caught by surprise when we used it. I heard a replay of the call the next day and Brooksie had done a great job. He was excited. "There goes Holieway to his left. He hands off to Jackson coming around. It's the 35, he's on his way to a touchdown. Jiminy Christmas!" That day Jackson ran three times for 130 yards as we beat Nebraska, 28-7.

The following year, Nebraska had us down by four points with about four minutes left. They needed to beat us at Lincoln in order to win the Big Eight Championship. Jackson was our go-to guy and it was time to go to him. On our winning drive, he made two miraculous catches, the last one an unbelievable one-hander that kept the drive alive. We pulled out a 17-14 victory and Switzer was beside himself. Later in the dressing room, still filled with emotion, he called Jackson's mother and told her how proud he was of her son. This was just one example of the spontaneous acts that Switzer would do from time to time.

Those same, wonderful years at Oklahoma we had a defensive player who generated more national publicity than anyone else I can remember on a college level. Brian Bosworth was known as the Boz and I never met a more colorful character. He had a funky hairdo that he peroxided, and he wore an earring. But he was a fantastic linebacker who always came to play. Switzer just let him be himself and he was a tremendous player who was focused and intense, very much like Lawrence Taylor. Everywhere we went that fall, all the media wanted to do was interview Brian.

I always referred to him as Brian. He was a good student, too. Sometimes he got out of hand, but he wasn't all that bad. He was fine as long as he was Brian, but when he turned into Boz, he became a personality and relished the spotlight. Nobody will ever know how good a pro he would have been. He played only two years for Seattle before a chronic shoulder ailment that required six operations ended his career.

Most pro fans remember Bo Jackson running over Bosworth for a touchdown in a Monday Night game, but Jackson could do that to anybody. I'm convinced that had Brian played just a couple more years he would have been an All-Pro. But he did all right financially. He wrote a book, had a ten-year guaranteed contract with Seattle, collected a million dollar insurance policy from Lloyds of London and made a movie. How many guys at 24 years of age can match that?

Just when I felt I found football heaven at Oklahoma, the sky caved in. Unfortunately, no one saw it coming. The entire program we worked so hard to build came tumbling down when three or four players broke NCAA rules and created a scandal that rocked the campus. The stories made headlines all over the country. Our recruiting had always been excellent because of the quality of athletes we went after. However, one year we took somewhat of a chance in signing some players who were marginal in the character area, kids who could prove troublesome and eventually did. Just like that, the OU football program was destroyed. Many good, innocent players suffered and Oklahoma lost its credibility.

No one suffered more than Switzer. The scandal forced him to resign, but in doing so he negotiated a settlement with the administration on his contract. Just before he left, Barry called the entire staff together and explained that the buyout and a retirement package was the only way and it was best for all of us if he left. It was a sad day, not only for OU football, but for the coaching staff as well. The Switzer era was over. I hadn't been a part of the program as long as most of the other assistants, but we all had been through so much together. We had clearly emerged as a national power, always a contender for the national championship. Now, suddenly, there was an empty, helpless feeling. I held back the tears when I met privately with Switzer.

"I just wanted you to know how much I appreciate what you've done for me and the program," sighed Switzer.

"Hey, the feeling is mutual. You've done a lot for me. I'm a better coach right at this moment than I've ever been."

"Well, you've lived up to every expectation I've had since the day I hired you. No one could ask for more than that."

"I enjoyed every minute of it. You were great to work for, an experience I can't put a value on. You've shown me what it takes to be a head coach."

"Look, the tougher times may be ahead."

"What could be worse than this? I still can't believe what happened."

"You're going to have to take charge and be loyal to Gary Gibbs because he'll probably be the one who'll replace me. But next year's team won't be as good as this one and everyone will start comparing you and Gary and everyone else to me."

"I suppose you're right in that regard. Who would ever have expected this?"

"It'll be a learning process and you'll have to act accordingly."

"It's not exactly something to look forward to. I mean, we're going from here to there. It wasn't supposed to be that way. It'll be interesting, to say the least."

"Jim, you have what it takes to be a head coach. If there is anything I can ever do to make it happen, just let me know."

I had faint hopes that I would be considered as Oklahoma's next coach. Nevertheless, Gibbs deserved it. He had been at Oklahoma longer, had played and graduated from there and did an outstanding job as defensive coordinator. The difficulty for Gary, and for all of us for that matter, was the negative publicity that would hang over us like a dark cloud.

Gary wanted to go in another direction, not only on a discipline level, but also in his football philosophy. He wanted to change from the wishbone to the I-formation, yet I didn't feel we had the personnel to make such an adjustment. I couldn't convince him otherwise. He felt that if we had a brand new look the comparisons to Switzer would be greatly diminished. I still didn't like it.

I wasn't comfortable with what I had to do and my final year at Oklahoma was very difficult for me. I wanted to be loyal to Gary and I was. All of us were feeling the heat following in Switzer's footsteps. In trying to please Gary, I made some coaching decisions we would have been better off doing another way. I felt we were going backwards offensively, trying to be something we couldn't be. We all learned that after the 1989 season, when we finished 7-4. It was the most losses we had in the five years I was at Oklahoma.

I learned from the situation and it helped me when I became a head coach. Barry said it would be a learning process and it was. I knew it was time to leave Oklahoma, although I had spent five great years of coaching there. If ever I was going to become a head coach, the time was now. The only disturbing part was that Todd was getting ready for his senior year in high school and Paige was engaged to Greg Johnson, one of our players. I knew it would be tough on my family to move again, but I felt a sense of desperation in my desire to become a head coach after 22 years in the game.

I began to explore my options, but there weren't many. I thought about calling Joe Paterno at Penn State. He had offered me a spot on his staff back in 1984. The complete opposite of Switzer, Joe is all football while Barry was not nearly as caught up in the day to day details. If you had the projector running and Barry came walking down the hall, he wouldn't bother to stop. He simply didn't enjoy the x's and o's as much as the interaction with the kids, whereas Joe would stop, look at the film and comment.

Joe is sincere and he didn't want to disrupt his staff when we talked in 1984. He wanted to add to it without affecting his other coaches. He cares about people and admitted that he was talking to other coaches also when he interviewed me. He disclosed that one of his assistants, Bobby Phillips, was retiring and that a spot would be available. Still, he was cautious.

Joe had a great amount of loyalty to his staff. He indicated that I was in a good position to join him at Penn State and we joked about the time he beat me as a player when we were going for our unbeaten season at North Carolina State. But the bottom line was that he didn't want to bring in a coach who would be on top of the others but rather one who would blend in. Knowing that, I preferred to stay at Missouri where I had more authority under Warren Powers. We led the Big Eight in offense three out of four years, beating Oklahoma twice in the process. Switzer never forgot that and he called and offered me a job.

Thinking back even further, I could have jumped to the NFL in 1983, when Parcells was the head coach of the New York Giants. In keeping the promise he had made to me when we were both at Florida State, he called and wanted me to learn the professional way as a special teams coach. I really didn't want that and because of my small town background I wouldn't be happy in a big city like New York.

When I was still at Missouri, I had a chance to go even further west, to Utah and Brigham Young University the same year Parcells called. It was serious enough for me to interview with Lavell Edwards. I liked him, but he was concerned how I would interact with the Mormon life-style and I appreciated his candor. While I was at Oklahoma, I had what I regarded as a strong possibility of becoming the head coach at the University of Wisconsin. However, they decided to go with a coach from the Midwest and hired Barry Alvarez from Lou Holtz's staff at Notre Dame.

I even thought about calling Wake Forest where I had a chance to go before Oklahoma, thinking it would be good to get back to my home state. My mind was racing with possibilities, when one thought kept coming back. Maybe I should have tried to become a head coach at a I-AA school instead of trying to be one in I-A.

My head was still spinning one cold day in January when Lee Moon, Marshall University's director of athletics, called. I hadn't spoken to him much since we had met in 1973, when he was an assistant coach at Duke. His phone call caught me by surprise. Lee made it clear at the beginning of our conversation he was looking for a new head football coach and was calling to find out if I was interested in interviewing for it.

"When?" I asked.

"How about tomorrow morning?"

I was silent for a moment.

"That fast, huh?"

"It has to be because I'm leaving Dallas in two days."

"Well, tomorrow morning it will have to be. I'll drive down and meet you at 6 o'clock."

I couldn't wait.

chapter 4 ►

ALONG CAME MARSHALL

The first thing that impressed me about Moon was his honesty during our phone conversation. I couldn't ask for anything more. Yet, during the three hour drive to Dallas, I kept asking myself, "Do I really want to take a step back to Division I-AA football?" The first ten minutes after I met Moon I knew I had to give him a quick answer. He was open and up front with me and disclosed that he had a short list of eight candidates. The more we talked, the more I became relaxed and I felt fortunate to be among those he had under consideration. We met for three hours and yet he didn't give any indication the job was mine if I wanted it. Nothing like, "If you accept, I won't talk to any of the other candidates." Most of the time we reminisced about our coaching days, which covered quite a few years.

"I received a recommendation from a friend of mine about you," began Moon.

"That's nice to hear," I smiled.

"The football job opened up just yesterday, but I had a feeling it was going to happen a few weeks earlier."

"In what way?"

"Jack Lengyel, the athletic director at the Naval Academy, told me that he had offered George Chaump the head coaching position and that he was going to take it."

"I understand. How serious a candidate am I for the Marshall job?"

"You're one of them. I have to settle on four of the eight names I have on my list."

"Well, let me leave you with this thought. I would like to be considered further. What I'm trying to say is that if you offer me the job, I'll accept it."

"I'll get back to you after I return from San Francisco."

I didn't feel good after hearing that. Suddenly, I felt a sharp pain in my gut, as if I had been hit with a quick punch. The NCAA coaches' convention was being held in San Francisco and my mind started imagining things. Wow, what an opportunity to go one on one with other coaches and liking enough of them to offer them the Marshall job. With all those coaches around, Lee certainly had the pick of the litter. Lots of times that's the way things happen. I could only hope this wasn't one of them.

Despite it all, I nevertheless had some good vibes driving back to Norman. I am a positive thinker and I wasn't about to start entertaining negative thoughts. I've always coached with a positive attitude and I've taken that course in life. Even though I didn't know the other candidates Moon had written down, I was comfortable feeling he at least knew me as a coaching adversary. The more I thought about it, the more I felt that my chances were improving.

When I was at North Carolina State, he was at Duke; when I was at North Carolina, he was at Virginia; when I was at Missouri, he was at Mississippi State; and finally, when I was at Oklahoma, he was at Kansas State. He was a defensive coach and I was on the offensive side, so in essence he knew my coaching philosophy. Why, there were even times when I recruited against him. I added all these factors in my mind and I was convinced they had to be advantageous for my chances of getting the Marshall job. I felt a lot better about the situation when I arrived home late that night.

There is nothing worse than waiting and not knowing what eventually will happen. My anxieties began the very next morning. I began to think of ways to enhance my chances but decided to let the decision rest on the interview. Looking back, if Lee wasn't seriously interested in me, we wouldn't have talked for three hours. However, he emphatically told me the final decision didn't rest with him but with the athletic committee. He emphasized that he would submit four names to the committee who would interview the four candidates before selecting a coach.

Thinking positively, I felt strongly that I would be one of the four. I decided that I wouldn't apply for any other coaching openings that were around, although there weren't too many left in January. If I didn't get a head job this year, then maybe my time would come next year. My son, Todd, still had another year remaining in high school and I resigned myself into thinking that perhaps it would be best if I didn't get the Marshall job. Whatever happened, I decided that Todd had to finish high school in Oklahoma.

Lee called me a week after he got back from San Francisco and told me what I wanted to hear. I was one of the four who would be interviewed by the Marshall Athletic Committee. I also found out who the others were: Rip Scheerer, the offensive coordinator at Arizona; Larry Blakeny, the offensive coordinator at Auburn; and Bill Clay, the offensive coordinator at Mississippi State. Who would have thought that Lee, a defensive coach all these years, would zero in on three offensive types. Moon went one step further. He confided in me that he felt that Scheerer and I were the front runners. I certainly appreciated hearing that.

I knew the interview would be the determining factor. On the way to Huntington, I remembered what Lee had said during our interview in Dallas. He was amazed that he had interviewed with 64 people in two days when he was an applicant for the Marshall athletic director position. He lost eight pounds because he was doing all those interviews and didn't have time to eat. What upset him wasn't so much the amount of people he had to face in the interviews, but the tone of the conversations that took place. All he heard during the interviews were complaints.

When he finally met with Marshall president Dr. Dale Nitzschke, he went on the offensive. I liked that. A defensive coach on the offense. He exclaimed to Nitzschke that he had just finished two interviews that consisted of 25 persons each, yet no one actually had interviewed him. All they did was gripe and complain about what wasn't being done at Marshall and how it couldn't be done. Then Lee went on the offense. He told Nitzschke a program can't be successful with that attitude and promised if he was hired, he would fire a bunch of those people. It was what Nitzschke wanted to hear. Moon got the job at that moment.

Considering what Lee went through, I was determined to come on strong during my interviews. I felt it was important that I presented positive thinking. I was scheduled for four interviews the two days I was in Huntington. Gary Gibbs knew of my decision in wanting to leave Oklahoma for a head coaching job and wished me luck, offering to help in any way he could. Now, it was strictly up to me and the impression I would leave with the athletic committee, which could be tough on coaching candidates. My only trepidation was that I would be prejudged as a wishbone coach.

Still, I approached the interviews with an open mind. I brought some highlight films to help dispel any doubts that I was a one dimensional coach who preferred the wishbone, one that featured the run. That false impression would be the only deterrent in my dossier because I felt that my knowledge of the area and my recruiting background in the South were beneficial. I looked upon it as a challenge. It's true that I had coached an offense at Oklahoma which led the nation in rushing, but I had coached an offense which led the country in passing, as well, when I was at Florida State.

With a quarterback like Troy Aikman and a tight end like Keith Jackson, I was primed for a big play offense at Oklahoma. Both were exceptional talents who come along every ten years or so. Troy had a strong arm and Keith was a big, strong end with speed. I was ecstatic drawing up pass patterns for what I felt could be one of the most explosive combinations I ever coached. But fate intervened. Aikman went down with a season-long injury and was replaced by Jamelle Holieway. It changed our entire offensive scheme. I had to revert from the pass to the run. Holieway was nowhere near the passer that Troy was. However, he was an excellent runner and

I utilized his strengths in our offense. He was quick with that first step and had good speed. I did the only thing I could and adapted to what Holieway presented on offense. I didn't have to sell Switzer on the theory of featuring Holieway on the run in our wishbone formation. We ran that offense the three years he played. And, those three years had stamped me as a wishbone coach.

That's why I was intent on bringing the highlight films with me to Huntington, to offset any doubts that the athletic committee members at Marshall may have had. I can cope with losing a game on the field but not one in a boardroom. I was faced with overcoming the reservations of some committee members that I was strictly a coach who ran the wishbone. While, on the contrary, I was hired at Oklahoma because Switzer remembered twice in the four years I was at Missouri our teams beat the Sooners. Switzer never forgot that. He wanted me to install a pro passing offense for Oklahoma and we were both excited about its prospects until Aikman got hurt.

I was aggressive during the interviews but was careful not to be too aggressive. I didn't want to turn anyone off. I really wanted the Marshall job even though it was stepping back to a I-AA program. I had my heart set on a I-A spot, but now my opportunities for getting a head coaching position were getting slim. The week before, I had interviewed for the Wisconsin job, which Moon was aware of and accommodated my schedule accordingly. I was appreciative and I told him so at the time. At Wisconsin, I was going up against a strong candidate in Barry Alvarez of Notre Dame. He had solid credentials and under Lou Holtz had helped build a winning program and a national championship.

It's funny how the Wisconsin interview came about. I had a kid from Wisconsin at my summer camp in Oklahoma. He was impressed at what he learned and that fall, after Wisconsin had another losing season, he got an appointment with Donna Shalala, the school president who is now Secretary of Education in the Clinton White House, and he told her about me. She, in turn, contacted the athletic director, Pat Richter, and he ultimately called me for an interview. It happened quickly, within three days, which didn't give me much time, to say the least. I went, although I felt it was a longshot. My intuition was right. They wanted someone from the Midwest who had a good knowledge of the Chicago area. So, Alvarez became the man for the job. Coming from Notre Dame, he was very familiar with Chicago and its big city newspapers. He certainly got the good press in 1993. Wisconsin won its first Big Ten Championship in years and topped it off with a victory over UCLA in the Rose Bowl.

I was much more confident after the Marshall interview was over. Moon confided I had made a good appearance and the committee seemed pleased. However, he cautioned me not to get too excited and told me that Scheerer would interview the next day. "I'll call you Wednesday night or Thursday morning," said Moon, when I left.

Sunday evening I left for the airport to return home to Oklahoma, wondering if I would finally get the chance to be a head coach. I wanted that more than ever.

Above With my parents, Jim and Runette, in 1945.

Left When I was six years old, I began playing my first organized sport - ping pong - and won the state championship each year until I was 18.

Following pages
(left) In high school, I decided to continue playing tennis instead of baseball and went on to win the state high school tennis championship.

(right) I played single wing tailback at Williams High School in Burlington, N.C.

1967 NORTH CAROLINA STATE VARSITY FOOTBALL TEAM

Front Row (Left-Right): Norman Cates, Billy Morrow, Harry Martell, Co-Captain Steve Warren, Co-Captain Art McMahon,
    Chuck Amato, Pete Sokalsky, Fred Combs.
Second Row: Don Donaldson, Jim Donnan, Lloyd Spangler, Trent Holland, Terry Brookshire, Dennis Byrd, Tony Barchuk, Greg Williams.
Third Row: Carey Metts, Jimmy Lisk, Gerald Warren, Ron Watkins, Mark Capuano, John McDuffie, Bobby Hall, Leon Mason,
    Flake Campbell.
Fourth Row: Settle Dockery, Benny Lemmons, Jack Klebe, Dick Schirippa, Art Waleski, Wayne Lewis, Mike Alford, Steve Diacont,
    Dick Idol, Bill Craig.
Fifth Row: Marvin Tharp, Paul Reid, Pete Bailey, Charles Tope, Gary Yount, Rocky Russell, Mike Hilka, Louis Biega, Dick Chapman,
    Kelly Jones.
Sixth Row: Brian South, Charlie Bowers, Jack Whitley, Jerry Miller, Bob Follweiler, Leroy Hamilton, Robby Evans, Don Jordan,
    Don Bullington.
Seventh Row: Steve Rummage, Darrell Moody, James Smith, Jim Hardin, Jerry Loftin, John Tranchese, Butch Altman, Dave Rodgers.
    Ron Harris, Marcus Martin.
Eighth Row: Rich Starodub, Art Hudson, Ron Carpenter, Andy Solonoski, Mike Joyce, Dick Vincich, George Botsko, Ed Nicholas,
    Pete Sowirka, Carleton Harrell.
Ninth Row: Coach Ernie Driscoll, Coach Al Michaels, Coach Bill Smaltz, Bill Williams, Jim Coman, Don Bumgarner, John Perotti,
    Reserve Zack Arthur, Reserve Billy Hart.
Back Row: Manager David Vaughn, Trainer Al Proctor, Coach Carey Brewbaker, Chancellor John T. Caldwell, Coach Claude Gibson,
    Coach Eugene Taylor, Wolfpack Club Director Warren Carroll, Equipment Manager Dorsey Poole, Head Coach Earle Edwards.

Far Left 1967 was a proud year for our N.C. State football team. We went 9-2 and won the school's first-ever bowl victory, a 14-7 win over Georgia in the Liberty Bowl. (I'm the second one from the left in the second row.)

Above & left At N.C. State, I played both quarterback and punter.

Following page Me posing with one of my favorite passing targets at N.C. State, end Harry Martel.

1967 Football Coaches and Players of the year

Football for 1967 has taken its last bad bounce, the season's records are history and the bowl scores are posted. Each season brings its joys and disappointments and produces its own crop of new stars and successful coaches. Here are the coaches and players of the year from the various regions chosen by our regional committees.

No claim is made that our selection is complete. We know that there are many other star players who performed brilliantly and that many other coaches are deserving of citation. Here are a few whom we are proud to invite into the spotlight for post-season recognition. These are not names drawn from a hat, but were chosen by committees of experts who were on the scene and made their choice after seeing the men perform on the field.

REGION	COACH	PLAYER
THE EAST	Joe Paterno, Penn State	Larry Csonka, Syracuse
ATLANTIC COAST	Frank Howard, Clemson	Jim Donnan, N. Carolina State
SOUTHEAST	Doug Dickey, Tennessee	Bob Goodrich, Vanderbilt
MIDWEST	John Pont, Indiana	Leroy Keyes, Purdue
MISSOURI VALLEY	Chuck Fairbanks, Oklahoma	Wayne Meylan, Nebraska
SOUTHWEST	Gene Stallings, Texas A & M	Edd Hargett, Texas A & M
ROCKY MOUNTAINS	Lloyd Eaton, Wyoming	Paul Toscana, Wyoming
PACIFIC COAST	John McKay, U.S.C.	Gary Beban, U.C.L.A.
		O. J. Simpson, U.S.C.

COACH & ATHLETE
MAGAZINE

Award

This certifies that

JIM DONNAN

N. CAROLINA STATE

has been named

PLAYER OF THE YEAR

in __Football 1967__

for __Atlantic Coast__
(Region)

Editor & Publisher

Presented
this __1st__
day of __February__
19 __68__

chapter **5** ▶

GOODBYE OKLAHOMA

W hat are you thinking?" Mary asked as I looked out the plane window, wondering if I would ever see Huntington again.

"About what?"

"Well, let's start with the Marshall job."

"I definitely want it."

"What do you think your chances are?"

"I feel pretty good about it, but you never know about interviews. A couple of people may not like you and that could be the end of it. There's nothing else I can do at this point."

"Did anyone give you any indication about how it went?"

"Not really. Nothing that I could build my hopes on. We'll just have to wait and see, but it won't be long. Moon said he'd call in a couple of days. I should know by Thursday."

Those were the longest three days of my life. Moon did call Thursday as promised. I held my breath as he began to speak. He came right to the point and congratulated me by offering the job if I still wanted it.

"Are you kidding, of course I do."

"Then you're the new Marshall football coach."

"It sounds good to me."

"We just have to work out the contract beyond the salary part."

"No problem there that I can see."

In the next fifteen minutes we tied up all the loose ends. I really couldn't be too demanding. After all, it was my first head coaching job. I did manage to get a television program and a radio show as part of the deal. I had learned a great deal about public relations and maintaining the right image from Switzer, including the role of TV and radio. I also stressed the importance of attending coaching clinics and public speaking engagements which was agreeable to Moon. He mentioned the area of fundraising through the Big Green Club and my participation with it. Just like Oklahoma, or any other institution for that matter, fundraising is a vital part of the athletic program.

Moon wanted to know when I could return to Huntington so he could introduce me at a press conference as the next Marshall coach. He emphasized the sooner the better, before the word of my appointment leaked out. I told him that I would get back to him the next day. There was something I had to do first that was a priority to me. I had to sit down with Mary and Todd and have a serious discussion now that I had a coaching opportunity. My accepting the Marshall job would have a direct bearing on both of them. Todd was finishing his junior year in high school and the thought of pulling him out his senior year troubled me. When he came home from school that afternoon, we sat and talked as a family. It was difficult for me. I finally became a head coach, something I worked hard for all these years and should have been in coaching heaven. I have always been a close family man and now I was presenting a situation that would split my family. I didn't like that. However, Todd made it easy for me.

"Dad, it's something you always wanted," he exclaimed.

"I know, but it's not the way I expected it. We've always been a close family, always together, and now this."

"Just go for it, Dad."

"That's easy to say, but what about you and Mom?"

"What about us?"

"For one thing, you're the captain of the team this season, and everyone is depending on you. I wouldn't want you to let anyone down."

"I won't be. I'll stay and finish high school here and Mom and I will join you after graduation."

"How does that sound to you, Mary?"

"I hate for all of us to be apart but there really isn't any other way."

"That's how I see it, too. It'll be rough on all of us for a while and I was just hoping there could be another way."

"What do you mean?"

"Well, maybe I was thinking a little selfishly. My dad's health isn't too good and since he lives in Charlotte, I was thinking how nice it would be for him to see me coach and see Todd play his final year of high school football. It was just a thought."

"Jim, as Todd put it, go for it. We're still a family and everything will be fine. Just don't go buying a house without me."

It was something we all wanted and within two days I was in Huntington to stay. Yet for the very first time in my life, I felt alone. I had never felt that way even as a child growing up in North Carolina. But when I signed the registration card that evening at the Radisson Hotel, I knew that this was where I would be living for the next year without Mary or Todd. Still, I got an empty feeling as I rode the elevator to my room. Oklahoma seemed a million miles away. Marshall Reynolds, who owns the hotel, made certain I wouldn't suffer from claustrophobia during my stay. He arranged for me to stay in a parlor suite overlooking the Ohio River. Not only did the suite have a bedroom, but it also had an adjoining room furnished with a large couch, a desk and a second television set. I had room to stretch and work.

I began the first of what would turn out to be a nightly ritual. I had promised Mary and Todd before I left that I would call them every night, and looking back, I must say I didn't miss too many. Another nightly routine I became occupied with was watching film, not the movies mind you, but football footage of Marshall's 1989 season. I would break down film practically every night even after viewing the same ones during the day at Marshall. I'm a big believer in studying film, running a play over and over to pick up anything that will give me an edge. When I do see an interesting play, I stop the film and mark it and go over the play with my coaches the next morning.

There's a fine line between winning and losing. Allie Sherman, the former New York Giants coach, once said that three key plays often determine the outcome of a game. I remembered that when I was playing at North Carolina State. He's accurate with that observation. Over the years I can recall hundreds of games and darn if those three plays didn't pop up and ultimately change the way the game turned out. That's why I study films so much, to find that something extra, and all the bleary-eyed hours I spent in a darkened room have paid off. Besides, this time I had another purpose in watching film. I had to get a line on our players since I never recruited any of them or saw them play. I had to make a staff evaluation before we ever got to the practice field.

In between, I made time to begin implementing my football philosophy which I formulated from all of my experiences, beginning the very first year I was an assistant coach at North Carolina State. I can sum up my philosophy in one thought, "to win." How do you make it happen? I believe it does not happen by chance. You control your own destiny by your attitude and those around you, together with how hard you are willing to work. Because of the late start in establishing a new program, I demanded long hours from the coaching staff I was beginning to assemble. I wanted an 8 AM start during the off-season and a 7:30 AM start during the season.

My one basic rule regarding office hours is to work long enough to get the job done. Coaches that try to beat the traffic home are usually coaches for a losing team, and I wanted no part of that. Yet, I had to be careful enough not to put a great deal of pressure on my staff during the off-season, as difficult as that first year appeared. We'd have enough of that during the long season ahead. I had to make certain my coaches didn't get involved in busy work which takes time and doesn't accomplish a great deal.

One thing I'm a stickler on is time. If there is any one thing that is perfectly equal to anyone it is time. I felt strongly about both our office and team being prompt. I called it "JD" time. I insisted that meetings and practices start on time. It develops a good work habit that both the coaches and the players can expect from one another. Above all else, loyalty has always been an asset to me and that had to continue. I expected my staff to be extremely loyal, not only to me, but to administrators, faculty, other coaches, players and office help. Loyalty is not just keeping quiet but also defending if the occasion occurs.

I also wanted a communicative staff, one that interacts with each other. If any problem arose, then I wanted my coaches to approach me and talk about it. I didn't want "yes" men. I wanted our staff to voice their opinions and suggestions on how we can get better. I was never one to place the blame. I only wish to correct the negatives which keep us from being successful. We must all be together trying for the same thing, to bring respect to Marshall football.

What I had to do quickly was hire a coaching staff. The easiest and best way was to bring in people that I was familiar with who believed in my coaching philosophy. I turned to Oklahoma and brought assistants I worked with, Chris Scelfo, Mark Gale, Tim Billings and Brad Lambert. I added Mickey Matthews from Southwest Texas State, whom I had known for 12 years. Naturally, my immediate concern was recruiting. As soon as I assembled the staff in Huntington, I assigned them territories and I went out myself in an effort to overcome a late start. It was almost February and we didn't have much time, less than a month to find and sign players.

Under the circumstances, my staff did an outstanding job. The first week alone we landed twenty prospects and lined up another four. I had only 18 scholarships to work with. The coaches were able to relate to the kids and that's important. I was particularly pleased that we competed and signed prospects from the state and the tri-state area which would help our recruiting in the future. The fact that we competed with West Virginia University for Chris Hamilton, and got him, was a big step for our program. LeRon Chapman, a running back at Huntington High School, is the type of player we would recruit at Oklahoma, big with a lot of raw talent that needed to be developed. We didn't have to go far to get him. He was in our backyard.

When it was all over, I would grade our first year recruiting efforts as a B. We helped ourselves on defense, both at linebacker and in the secondary. We also added some talent in the skill areas. I was disappointed that we didn't get as many linemen as we hoped but defensive linemen are like dinosaurs, hard to find. I decided to put off the search for help on the junior college front because with the late start we faced, the good ones were already gone to schools to take part in spring drills. As such, our spring practice was beginning late, April 2, and ending with the annual Green-White game on April 28, when the semester was almost over.

Yet, I discovered that a football fan in Norman is no different than a football fan in Huntington and that first month of recruiting reminded me of it. In

Oklahoma, they've all got opinions and Huntington appeared to be even more opinionated. It seemed everyone I met had a suggestion. They all wanted to be in the know and tell you how things should be done. I had more coaches out there than players. It's what being a fan is all about, I guess. I was just amazed at the similarities between a big school and a smaller one. Regardless of the level, athletics is a big show and everyone wants to be a part of it. But for the most part, I found them receptive even though some of them felt I talked too slow. I was comfortable with the feeling that they felt good about our involvement. I knew they would be looking at us closely after the success they experienced under George Chaump.

Nevertheless, I still felt their apprehension about the brand of football I brought with me. Chaump directed this team and did it well for four years, reaching the championship game one year. He's an excellent coach and his record proved it. But he coached for Woody Hayes at Ohio State and didn't exactly come in here and run a three yards and a cloud of dust type of offense. Yet, I have to be me. I can't be George Chaump, or Barry Switzer for that matter. I learned from Switzer that you play talent, not experience. Whatever talent I discover between spring and fall practice, we'll go with, be it the run or the pass. You don't win with formations. Rather, you win with blocking and tackling and skill players and I'm flexible to the point of running the football or passing it, whatever it takes to win.

All I was asking for was a chance and not to be prejudged on what was or wasn't going to happen. I knew we would put points on the board and make it exciting. I was also convinced of one other point. We can be on the same level in our division that Oklahoma is in Division I-A. That was one of my goals and I surrounded myself with people I had confidence in, who felt the same way, who can coach football, can teach and recruit good student-athletes to make the program successful. I told Lee Moon if I didn't think we could be the best in the country, I wouldn't have taken the job, but remained at Oklahoma instead.

Leaving Oklahoma was very emotional for me. I had to say goodbye to a lot of friends. But more importantly, I had to leave Mary and Todd. Yet, everybody was happy for me. Like Todd remarked, it's something I always wanted. He was right.

chapter **6▶**

BUSY DAYS, LONELY NIGHTS

I was getting anxious. Maybe my solitary hotel life had something to do with it. I wasn't sleeping much and I was socializing even less. But after watching so much film I wanted to see the players on the practice field and get the program where I wanted it to be. My time alone had made me into more of a workaholic than I already was. The one good thing was that it allowed me to spend more time privately with each player. I wanted to know them and at the same time let them know where I was coming from. Like Bill Parcells, I shared his belief in being a player's coach. And what better way than to go one-on-one with each of them. I told every player that I talked to the first two months that my door was always open to them. If they had a problem, personal, class, work, football related or whatever, I was available to help them.

After studying films of the 1989 games, I was convinced that I wouldn't be running the wishbone. I didn't have the personnel. It was as simple as that. I remained firm in my belief that we'd run what our players can do well, and spring practice would help determine that. I knew that I would be taking Marshall in a new direction. I felt strongly about getting it done and repeated to any doubters not to make rash judgments.

I wasn't about to defend to anyone the way we were going to play football. Although this was my first head coaching opportunity, I had absorbed all I could as an assistant from all the stops along the way. My fulfillment occurred in the last five years at Oklahoma. We were 49-10 during those years and won 27 straight Big Eight games. The ultimate was the national championship following an 11-1 season and our victory over Penn State, 25-10, in the 1986 Orange Bowl. I knew I was ready to be a head coach.

That memory drove me. The overall success at Oklahoma allowed me to think big in wanting to take Marshall to that level. I was happy I was here and I could see by all that was happening that it was a good fit. With a new 30,000 seat stadium opening in 1991, I knew Marshall officials were committed to reaching the championship level. It was up to me to get them there and I welcomed the challenge. I remembered the quote that Switzer made in *The Herald-Dispatch* after I got the Marshall job: "I hired Jim in 1985 and he took us to the national championship." It reminded me I wanted another one.

I didn't quite know how quickly a championship could be achieved, however. But I was willing to work hard in making it happen as quickly as possible. The first year was critical. I instructed my staff to look for players that were coachable. The returning players that I talked to understood what we were trying to accomplish with a new staff and a new system. I found them receptive the very first day I called them together as a group. They had been successful to a degree and now they were sitting out there with a bunch of coaches they didn't know. We had to gain their trust. Coming from a winning program made it easier to accept us and what we were trying to do as a team.

I had a couple of areas of concern. One was the practice facilities at Fairfield Stadium. Although the playing field itself was adequate, the locker room facilities were inferior. They were small and crowded, and I shuddered at the thought of seventy or so bodies in one place. Besides, it was an inconvenience that translated into lost time. We were on the east end of town so we had to line up for buses for practice on the other end and we didn't exactly have roomy Greyhounds for our travel. But it wasn't intolerable to the point that it was upsetting. I knew it was only temporary. I kept thinking of next year when the new stadium on the campus would be completed and with it, state-of-the-art facilities, including classrooms, workout rooms, locker rooms and coaching offices all under one roof.

What was more of a concern was the physical condition of the players. In my eyes it was heartbreaking. There wasn't a budget for a full-time strength coach and it showed on the kids. Most had upper body strength but that's all. They had no flexibility, team speed or quickness, because obviously it was never worked on. The offensive line never had any strength base, no direction whatsoever. There was nothing in the area of leg strength, flexibility, conditioning and endurance. Now, I never expected this. I would have to start from scratch with a weight program for each player.

I'm a great believer in a weight program and now I found myself without one. I knew of only one way to handle it and that was to call in a favor and I did so by phoning Scott Reese in Oklahoma. I had known him since 1987 when he came to the university as the assistant strength coach. I knew he would help.

"Scott, I need you," I began.

"What's up, coach?"

"I have a big problem, one I didn't anticipate. The physical condition of this team is terrible. There's no strength coach, no weight program, nothing. The players just lift on their own."

"What do you want me to do?"

"Scott, I can't even offer you a job at this point because there's no money in the budget for a full-time strength coach. But you've got to help me until I can find some money somewhere and you know the job will be yours if you want it."

"Let's go one step at a time. We'll worry about the job down the road. What do you need now?"

"I need you to outline a strength and conditioning program for the entire team, quarterbacks, running backs, receivers, linemen, defensive backs, you name it."

"How fast do you need it?"

"Like a month ago."

"Is it really that bad?"

"Scott, I start practice in two weeks and I need to have it in place by then."

"You just ruined my weekend. I was going to Texas but now I have to work. Tell you what. I'll work up some basic stuff and Fed Ex it to you on Monday morning just to get you going. The ideal situation would be a hands-on approach so I could look at every kid and offer individual attention. But as I mentioned, that's down the road."

"I'd love to have you here for a visit. I have to insist on the importance of a full-time strength coach so don't sign any long-term contracts until you hear from me."

"You got it."

By July we came up with some money in the budget for a strength coach. I brought Scott in for the job I promised him. I almost lost him the very same day. He wasn't sure he wanted to leave Oklahoma once I picked him up at the airport and showed him the facilities. He was ready to go back on the next plane.

"You have to be kidding, coach," he remarked.

"I told you I need help and you're the one to do it."

"But the weight room is so small and run-down. Even the equipment is inadequate, no maintenance of the weights. This is one helluva job to do."

"Don't concern yourself with now as much as next year. Let me show you the plans for the new facilities. You'll have the opportunity to design and equip a brand new weight room with a full-time program."

"You brought me all the way from Oklahoma for this? That'll cost you a pair of boots."

"Then you'll do it?"

"You hooked me. Yes, I'll do it although I think I may be a little crazy."

Reese was just one of the coaches who made sacrifices in coming to Marshall. Tim Billings had probably made the biggest sacrifice. He had worked with me for two years at Missouri, and when I got the offensive coordinator job at Oklahoma, I took him with me to coach the fullbacks. Ironically, he coached Leon Perry, who later joined us as a running back coach at Marshall. Tim wasn't a full-time coach at Oklahoma only because the football budget didn't provide for one. After a year, he returned to Missouri and coached tight ends for two years. He came here at an emotional time in his life. His wife had given birth to a premature girl who was only six days old and still in an incubator when he left. I couldn't ask for more out of anybody.

Chris Scelfo, Mark Gale, Mickey Matthews and Brad Lambert also sacrificed. I had to assemble a staff practically overnight and I didn't give anybody much time to make a move. Gale didn't even know where Marshall was and Scelfo guessed it was in Pennsylvania, confusing it with Franklin & Marshall. I told them they only had time to pack just a couple of suitcases because Moon was flying in the next morning on an Ashland Oil company jet to bring us to Huntington. The flight took a bit longer than expected because of the rain we encountered along the way.

Gale got a big kick out of the reception we received at the airport. He saw so many green jackets that he thought he was at the Masters. Then, when people walked up to us and carried our bags, Gale smiled.

"I'm going to like it here, Coach," he whispered.

"Me, too," added Scelfo.

Matthews joined us that evening after flying up from Texas. I first met him in 1978 at Kansas State when I was the backfield coach and he was a graduate assistant. He left to go back to Texas after two years, but we kept in contact over the next twelve years. Down deep, Mickey was a frustrated cowboy. I might not have convinced him to leave Texas if the timing hadn't been right. There was a big coaching shake-up at Southwest Texas State which cost the head coach, Jon O'Hara, his job. They wanted Mickey to stay, but he didn't like what had taken place.

Lambert was the youngest of the five. I liked what I saw in him while he was a graduate assistant my final two years at Oklahoma. I couldn't offer him a full-time salary but promised him one in a year when the budget would be better. I explained that he could advance faster in the coaching profession if he came along. He worked on defense at Oklahoma and I felt he would work well under Matthews with the defensive ends. We were set with a great deal of work ahead of us. The other coaches I hired were Fred Manual from Louisville and a long-time friend of mine, Joe Dickinson from Tulsa.

I was up at five o'clock the day spring practice began. I couldn't sleep, thinking about the day. This was my first practice as a head coach and I was eager to see the assembled team on the field in pads. That morning I went over every detail with my coaches. First impressions are important and I didn't want to leave anything undone. We met for three hours then broke for lunch. After the hour break, we reviewed everything we discussed in the morning session. As fate would have it, rain greeted us on the practice field. I barely noticed.

My first act was to gather the players around me. I wanted to clear the air and start fresh. An after-hours incident involving two players had occurred and I didn't want to start like that. I quickly learned after I got here that there were a couple of late night spots that made Route 60 attractive to party goers. I was emphatic in making it known that it was off-limits to every member of this football team. I was firm but understanding. I realized the players might have felt some insecurity, a sense of abandonment following the departure of the coaches who had recruited them. This isolated incident by two players was a sign of releasing frustration. Time would remedy that.

I didn't know much about their skills, except what I had seen on film. Yet, I felt the receivers and running backs were the strongest positions. The one position I had to establish was quarterback. That's the first question everyone asks: who's going to be the quarterback? I had seven listed but I was in no hurry to make a judgment. It wasn't necessary to establish someone in the spring. I always look to fall practice because it gives more time with two-a-days. A team can get nearly as much done in one week in the fall as in all of spring practice. You can get in a lot more repetitions and you have more time to experiment in the fall. I'm not a believer of a two-quarterback system. My timetable was to have an established quarterback by the week of our first game, and I wasn't going to rush into it.

By now I had put away the wishbone fears by starting with an I-formation and branching out. I repeated to the squad our philosophy that formations and alignments don't win for you; blocking and tackling do. My aim was to have a balanced attack while putting a premium on getting better in short yardage and goal line situations. I didn't feel we had the capabilities of a big play offense with the players that were lost from the previous year. The guy that made it happen at quarterback, John Gregory, was gone after setting passing records that caught my eye. In three years he passed for 7,020 yards and 51 touchdowns. I sure would have loved to have had that going into my first season.

Still, we inherited a winning program and the atmosphere that went with it. The players were used to winning and expected to win. They had been well coached and we were not starting entirely from scratch. Yet, it was up to us to sell them on a new program. I truly didn't anticipate any problems in doing so. My coaches, too, were used to winning and it would show in their teaching. Kids can pick up quickly on that.

The first major change we wanted was on defense and the installation of a 4-3-4. We all felt that the personnel we had on defense would be more effective with only two down linemen and two stand-up ends. That setup would enable us to get more interaction between our ends and linebackers in compensating for the weakness of the line. We determined that we had more end-linebacker types and had to make use of them. We already had decided before we got on the practice field that we would switch Mike Gill from offensive guard to defensive tackle to help us there.

I wasn't too concerned about the offense. Yes, Gregory was a big loss, but there were enough candidates at the quarterback position and if numbers meant anything, I was rich. Two of the seven had some experience, Michael Payton and Gregg Supsura. I wasn't going to determine the starter until fall anyway, preferring to promote competition. My biggest worry was finding a running back to replace Ron Darby, the school's all-time career rusher with 3,903 yards. He indeed was a premium player, one that doesn't come around often. Yet, I liked what I saw on film of Orlando Hatchett and felt he could be the answer. Two others that I had high hopes for were tight end Eric Ihnat and wide receiver Andre Motley.

But I never worry about what we lose, just the ones we have coming back. That's why you recruit. There's always somebody ready to take over and I have to find them. They just need the chance. That's what happened at Oklahoma. Aikman went down for the year and Holieway, a freshman, took over a new offense and led us to the Big Eight Championship. Even though I had formulated some early opinions about some of the players from watching film, this first spring with them was important.

I couldn't truly judge skill levels until now. We had to identify our best athletes and get them on the field, teaching them our system while being flexible enough in not asking them to do something they couldn't. I had only three weeks to do it in. The whole period would be a crash course and I was hoping to have the twenty best days possible to look over 87 players and find the answers. Only then, when we could evaluate the amount of talent, could we finally determine what offense would best fit our personnel.

After the first week I was pleased with the progress we made. Our top priority was to find out who could get off the blocks. We started off by putting in six running plays, eight pass plays and our base defense. The attention and enthusiasm were remarkable and I was thrilled that they adjusted to what we were trying to do without any difficulty whatsoever. The defense was aggressive and showed good techniques, but we still had a long way to go.

The one cumbersome spot was at quarterback. Seven sounds good but it was too many to work with. I was willing to give them all a chance, just to see what happened. Supsura had been around as a back-up to Gregory, yet Payton was an excellent athlete. The ideal situation was to concentrate on two. Supsura was hampered by a sore shoulder, which gave Payton an opportunity to take more reps with the first team offense. I liked his scrambling ability while maintaining accuracy with his passing.

After the Green-White game, I sat down with my staff to evaluate our first spring practice. We were pleased with the way the kids picked up on what we were trying to do. Our long hours of hard work and extra scrimmages paid off. I, for one, was impressed with the attitude displayed by the players. In the first three weeks we had an enormous amount of contact in an attempt to see how the players reacted. We also made progress with mental discipline. We can talk at length about it but the players have to get on the field to experience it. We didn't kid ourselves. There were still a great many hours of work to do before fall practice. We had to do a better job on offense, and Hatchett gave signs that he could come up big by then. The defense played the run okay but needed to improve against the pass. Overall, the team's speed wasn't good enough and had to improve.

There is no discounting how hard we worked. Some of the players quit while some weren't sure what they wanted to do. Fortunately, we were able to get across to them how important it was to make sacrifices and to be a part of a team. We had less talent than I thought we would have, and I attributed the shortage to the fact that recruiting had been weak since George Chaump had been in his final season.

Much of that first spring was made easier through the cooperation and guidance I received from Don Williams. He was an ex-football coach who was a member of the athletic committee and understood what I was going through. Along with Lee Moon, he gave me the most help. Don led me through some choppy waters and helped me build solid relationships. It was an easier transition because of his help.

That first year I wanted to build a foundation for Marshall's football future and felt that one way to do so was to start a football camp for the area's high school players. I scheduled it for July, a month before our players reported for fall practice. The freshmen were scheduled for August 7 and the veterans five days later. The camp also allowed our staff the opportunity to meet many high school coaches who could be instrumental in our recruiting efforts.

By this time in the summer all of the staff was getting antsy. We had some of the players in town on weightlifting programs and Scott Reese worked extra long hours from the first day he arrived. I still owed him a pair of boots.

"I should have stayed in Oklahoma," he groaned.

"Why, this is a piece of cake for you," I answered.

"It will be, once we get the new facilities, so I can run a first-rate program for these kids. They're willing enough. I don't have the space or all the equipment I need. That's what makes it so tough."

"Well, do the best you can with what you have. It'll still be better than what was here."

All the more reason the building of a new stadium and the facilities it offered were important. By next year it would provide the program with a whole new meaning. When I first arrived at Marshall, I felt strongly about taking the program from I-AA to I-A. However, I could see by now it was going to take a bit longer than I expected. Realistically, we had to walk before we could run. We had to beat the teams in our conference. Coming in here, the talent wasn't what I thought it was. I didn't feel we could beat any Division I schools with what we had. I knew we couldn't. There's a big difference between playing North Carolina State and having a chance to beat them instead of merely lining up against them just to make the schedule more attractive and make money for the nonrevenue sports.

But I was determined. I wasn't interested in spending four or five years just to be competitive. I wanted to go out and win. That's what I'm used to doing. You show me a good loser, and I'll show you a loser, period. This was my first year as a head coach and I was going to make it the best one I could. I had a staff that was dedicated and it was up to all of us to bring in the right kids, ones with both character and ability. I went through a bad experience one year at Oklahoma with a bad group of athletes who destroyed our program and all we had accomplished. I don't ever want to go through that again.

The experience was a stunning reality. No one was expecting it. I realized there is only one alternative once the mistake has been made - learn from it. Sometimes the reins are too tight and sometimes they're too loose. We learned that we needed to tighten them up a little bit more at Oklahoma. In one four-day period we had a rape, a shooting and a drug arrest. That's why character is an important attribute of any athlete we recruit. You can't win with bums and I was not going to tolerate bad behavior, regardless of how good a player was.

My first concern when we started spring practice was the senior players on the team. They weren't recruited by us and we certainly were not going to come in right off the bat and say, "Hey, we're going to start building a new program with all new, young players." This was their team and we wanted to make sure that they would have a good senior year. That's why we were going to give them the first opportunity at every position. Still, I also believe in playing the talent, regardless of the experience. At Oklahoma, we won a national championship with a freshman quarterback. I don't believe you have to have experience to be successful. You have to have the talent, first and always.

At the start of fall practice, I had several problems which had to be solved. The first was the lack of a proven quarterback and the other a lack of defense. In other words, I had major concerns on both sides of the ball. Unfortunately, my troubles didn't end there. I was concerned also about the lack of team speed by the veteran members of the squad. We had to supplement the old with the new. We had over a hundred players, including the walk-ons, and it was up to us to filter out the best from the rest in the three weeks before the season-opener.

Brian Dowler, Ricardo Clark and Andre Motley provided us with good talent at wide receiver and I was set on throwing the ball a lot. It would depend on us having someone to get them the ball consistently. I was looking for someone who could make the big play. Going in, Payton had the edge over Supsura. He had a good arm, not what I consider a great one, but he also possessed good mobility, which you can't teach, and I was impressed with his running ability. Payton had decent size at 6-1, 208, and he had made a lot of strides since I had seen him in the spring. The more I watched him, the more I became convinced he could become an excellent quarterback with his above average speed and arm.

The other receiver I felt could contribute was tight end Eric Ihnat. In fact, I was heavily depending on him. Our other tight end, Mike Bartrum, whom I expected big things from, sustained a knee injury during our spring game. It was worse than we had first thought, and he was lost for the entire 1990 season. That was a big blow to our offense. But from what I could see of Ihnat, he had the makings of a pro prospect. The staff felt he could become a I-AA All-American in his final season. As far as the running game went, I smiled with the thought of Orlando Hatchett. He was the star of the spring game, and although he was only a sophomore with limited playing experience, I saw big play potential in him. He could have played at Oklahoma and that's probably one of the highest compliments I could give him.

We discovered some good young players, once fall practice began, that made me feel much better about our defense. Jim Bernadoni, a freshman at defensive end, was one of them. Freshmen defensive backs Shannon Morrison and Joe Chirico were two more. I was beginning to feel confident that we might be able to surprise some people. The biggest task was replacing four starters up front. We had to make a lot of changes there. One of the biggest was switching Phil Ratliff from tackle to offensive guard, taking a sophomore with experience and leaving us thin. But we felt we had some good young prospects to make our 4-3 defense work, even with a relatively inexperienced secondary. I liked the looks of William King, a freshman from Charleston, and moving Derek Grier from safety to cornerback would allow him to make more plays. I didn't have to worry about a kicking game. Dewey Klein had already set a Marshall record with 31 field goals, and he was only a junior.

We were fortunate to get Shannon King, a local product from Huntington. He was actively recruited by West Virginia, Wake Forest and Virginia Tech, all major schools. I was surprised by what he told me, that the previous Marshall coaches didn't recruit anybody in the Huntington area. That made my idea for a summer camp all the more important. King came in as a running back and that's how we listed him, but I wasn't quite sure that was his best position. The first time he sat in front of my desk he appeared a bit timid.

"What's wrong, son?"

"I kind of like your ring," he beamed.

"You do, huh?"

"It's a beauty all right."

"That's what you get when you become a national champion like we did at Oklahoma."

"I wouldn't mind getting one of those."

"Tell you what. If you come to Marshall, I promise you'll be wearing one of these rings."

"That's something to think about."

"Well, it's up to you. If you make your grades on your SAT's, I'll take you and give you that chance."

The one thing I was reminded of was that Marshall had a record of five straight winning seasons going into 1990. I certainly didn't want to be remembered as the one who broke it my first year. I thought about our chances. I felt we could win six or seven of our eleven games. The way I analyzed it, if we won our first two games, were competitive on the road and then won two of the remaining five at home, we could do just that.

I left a final thought with my players the final day of fall practice. I called it Donnan's Law. It consisted of one basic rule simply put, "If it's right, do it; if it's wrong, don't do it." I concluded with a warning that any player who cares to test me on this will find out how quickly I'll act. Here's how fast. Take a cup of water, pour it through your hands and watch it hit the ground. That's about how long I'll miss somebody who doesn't follow the rules.

All that was left now was to open the season and see what kind of football team we were. A team consisting of coaches and players who, only six months earlier, were strangers to one another.

chapter 7 ►

1990 SEASON

I was sure of one thing, we'd be an exciting team. What I wanted to do on offense was a bit different. I wanted to pass to set up the run rather than the opposite, which was more conventional. I had that much confidence in Payton. He rapidly progressed from spring ball by working hard all summer in seizing the opportunity to start ahead of Supsura, who was a senior. Once more my philosophy of playing talent ahead of experience played a big part in making Payton the starting quarterback. Besides, he demonstrated during fall practice that he had earned it. That's the time of year it's happening and I watched him closely.

He had ability all right, but I had to instill confidence in him. When he was recruited, he was told that he could probably be a starter as a freshman. He threw the ball a lot his senior year in high school in Pennsylvania and was heavily recruited by a number of I-A schools. In his first season at Marshall, he handed off the ball more than he passed. When he was asked to throw, he looked awful because he wasn't ready for it. He didn't have consistency. A week before we opened the 1990 season against Morehead, I called Payton into my office.

"Michael, you're the number one," I said flatly.

"I appreciate your confidence in me, Coach," he answered.

"Look, you've earned it. The staff feels the same way I do. Just forget about last season. You have three years ahead of you and just make the most of them."

"You bet I will. I had been a little down on myself after last year."

"I knew that. But that's all over with now. I'm giving you the ball and I want you to make things happen out there. We have the makings of a good team and I need a quarterback to make it go. You're the one who can do it. It's a first year experience for all of us and a fresh start for you."

"I'll make the most of it."

I had to make the most of an offense that hadn't established an identity yet from what I could see in the short time we had been together. In retrospect, it was Payton's first full season after a redshirt year that had shaken his confidence. I wasn't going to confuse him, and the rest of the offense for that matter, with a lot of formations. We were going to operate out of the I and a one-back set. Ideally, I didn't want to pass more than 35 times a game. Any more than that only meant that you'd be throwing out of necessity. Perfection to me would be a 50-50 run-pass offense, but it rarely comes out that way.

I wasn't counting too heavily on the deep pass. Rather, it was our intent to nickel and dime the ball down the field, which helps control the clock while building confidence in Payton. The key for him to recognize on defense was an area around the line of scrimmage we called the box. If there are seven defenders there, they are playing the run. If only six appear, then they are looking for the pass. Naturally it dictates what calls the quarterback makes, especially in checking off. With Payton, we figured to be option oriented and feature the short to medium range pass. With Hatchett, Pedro, Clark and Ihnat, we could do a lot of things without substituting, an advantage in itself because you can force the defense into problems.

Our schedule was among the more difficult in the country. Fortunately, we had six home games and it meant a great deal, from what I heard about the Marshall tradition. It centered around the fact that Marshall had lost only one game at Fairfield Stadium the past three seasons. I wasn't concerned about how many times Marshall had beaten Morehead, our first opponent of the season, over the years. My interest was in my first game as a head coach.

Morehead had worked a bit of psychology on us in the weeks before the game. The season before, they had used the I-formation exclusively. However, under new coach Cole Proctor they were sending the word out that he would employ the wishbone. There's that word again. We didn't know what to expect but knew they had a quarterback, Chris Swartz, who set school and Ohio Valley Conference passing records. That's quite an accomplishment when you consider that Phil Simms, who's played quarterback for the New York Giants, played at Morehead.

I didn't remember it being this hot in Oklahoma during football season. At game time it was 86 degrees - at night! I was glad it wasn't a day game. You would be looking at a field temperature of over 100 degrees and that's a problem for any team, conditioned or not. I looked around the stands expecting a capacity crowd for my first game, but I guess the unusual heat kept several thousand people away on the river or at the beach. Besides, I learned in the spring that people love their golf around here, and I'm sure there were a lot of them still on the links at seven o'clock.

I was thinking, wouldn't it be wonderful if we won the coin toss, got the ball first, and went the length of the field for a touchdown? What an exciting way for a coach to begin his career. Instead, Morehead had the first shot and made me sweat a little too early. Nothing serious, as I look back, but when you're coaching your very first game, everything becomes magnified. What had me a little uneasy was that Morehead converted their opening two first downs on third down plays. That's not a good sign. But we got the ball back and I let out a sigh.

I couldn't have drawn our first two plays any better. I wanted to get Payton off fast and he did, with a 16-yard completion to Hatchett. Then Hatchett ran up the middle for 15 yards. Two plays, 31 yards. I thought I was back in Oklahoma. But that was it for the moment. We had to kick and I had to wait for my first touchdown. Fortunately, I didn't have to wait long. We got the ball right back in good field position on the Morehead 43.

Again we called a first down pass and Payton hit Motley for nine. Hatchett carried for eight and a first down. Payton threw again, this time to Clark for eight more. We kept Morehead off balance with a run and Hatchett made 12 to the six-yard line. I was thinking touchdown and feeling good. I wanted Payton on the option. When he fumbled, I held my breath until he recovered. We stuck with him. He got five yards on a keeper to the one. Third down and just a yard away. I was anxious. Give it to him once more, I ordered. He scored and that one yard felt like a hundred.

In the second quarter we scored again. This time Payton did it with a pass. He hit Clark with an 18-yarder for a 14-0 lead. I felt in control at halftime with the knowledge that we would get the second half kickoff. We had moved the ball well in the first half, and if we could continue to do so with the second half kickoff, we could put Morehead in a hole. The way our defense was playing, it would be difficult for Morehead to come back.

Well, we helped them. On the second play of the half, Payton made a mistake. He misread the defense and his pass was intercepted on the 35-yard line and run back for a touchdown. The cushion we enjoyed at halftime was gone and our offense went three and out in the next series. When Morehead reached our 35, I was beginning to fear a change in momentum. But Donahue Stephenson, our middle linebacker, came up with a big play by recovering a fumble on the 36-yard line.

The next offensive series was big, in my eyes. We needed a spark and freshman fullback Glenn Pedro gave it to us. He brought the crowd to its feet and the players jumping up and down the sidelines with a 57 yard run straight up the middle. I didn't think he would get caught but he got pulled down on the three. I tried to get him the touchdown with two runs but he got only one yard each time. On third down I called Payton's number and he went around right end for the touchdown that restored our 14 point lead, 21-7.

We couldn't seem to shake Morehead. Early in the fourth quarter they scored again on a long drive and trimmed our lead to 21-14. My anxieties quickened on the kickoff when we fumbled and Morehead recovered on our 41 yard line. They got a bit eager. They tried to score quickly with the pass but completed only one for three yards. Still, we kept helping them out. Payton made another bad throw that was intercepted on our 32. I was beginning to think, what is going on here, when Stephenson came up with another big play, an interception.

I told Payton and the offense to settle down when they went back on the field. We worked the ball for over five minutes on a 65-yard drive which Payton finished by scoring his third touchdown. At 28-14, with two minutes left, I was assured of my first Marshall victory. I'll never forget it. The players knew how much it meant to me and gave me the game ball. I responded that this was only the first and that from this moment on, I wanted to be the one handing out the others. Mary had flown in to see my head coaching debut, and I couldn't wait to call Todd back in Oklahoma. He knew the moment he answered and heard my voice that we had won.

Payton demonstrated why we decided to play him. He responded to the challenge and established himself as the quarterback by showing a lot of athletic ability. He threw the ball well, and even though he made a couple of mistakes, they were correctable. I knew we'd get better as the season went on. I had a quarterback and a young defense that hung tough.

I was beginning to wonder if it ever gets cold in Huntington. When we played West Virginia Tech the following week, it was 82 degrees. And that was the nighttime temperature. Tech was an NAIA school and I didn't expect much of a challenge. Neither did the fans. Not that many showed up, about 14,000. I approached the game as a learning process for all of the team. We had players we needed to know about and if the game went the way I expected, everyone would get a chance to play. Tech coach Jim Marsh saw us against Morehead and left impressed. He remarked that we didn't look like a team that was in the process of rebuilding. I certainly hoped he was right.

By half-time the game was over. We jump-started a 14-0 first quarter lead to 45-0 at half in our easy 52-0 victory. After the first period, I pulled the first team defense to look at others who could provide us with depth as the season progressed. After the opening drive in the third period, the first team offense was finished for the night. I've never been one to run up scores. I wasn't worried about the game as much as I was about looking sloppy. The only worry afterwards was injuries to tackle Chris Deaton and defensive back Shannon Morrison.

We had a week off before leaving for Charleston, South Carolina, to play The Citadel. I was looking forward to it. It gave me the opportunity to go back to Norman and see Todd play for the first time as a quarterback. Marshall Reynolds made his private jet available and I couldn't thank him enough. The week off was welcomed by the coaching staff, too. The Citadel was the first of three Southern Conference opponents and we didn't know much about our league rivals. Heaven knows, though, I knew about The Citadel's wishbone offense and their quarterback Jack Douglas. He had gained 154 yards on the ground and 107 yards more in the air for 261 yards of total offense the week before. Our thinking was to defend the wishbone inside out by stopping the fullback. Patience was the word we used with the players. They had a high risk offense and odds were they would make errors in execution.

Well, we made the mistakes, not them. My first loss was a frustrating one, 21-10. I couldn't imagine gaining 445 yards and scoring only one touchdown, on a fake field goal no less. Our defense was wonderful, holding The Citadel to 200 yards, but our offense had three fumbles and three interceptions and I had a giant headache. Five times we moved into scoring position during the second half only to come up empty.

That didn't give me a good feeling about playing Furman, although the game was in Huntington. We respected Furman. We spent the entire month of May working on them by breaking down films of the 13 games they played in 1989. We figured they were the best team in our conference and spent most of the off-season preparing for them. That's how much we respected them - we viewed the Furman game as a critical matchup before the season even started.

It was the end of September and the temperature was 78 degrees. I'm thinking, something is wrong here. Maybe I'm back in the Orange Bowl playing Miami. No, not quite, but Furman was enough. They had a sophomore running back named Carl Tremble who gained 987 yards as a freshman. They had won 13 straight conference games which explained why they were picked to win the title again. They lined up in the I and with Tremble as the featured back, were averaging 244 rushing yards a game. Those were Oklahoma numbers.

Although Dewey Klein gave us a 36-yard field goal at the start of the game, I knew it wasn't enough. Furman scored on a pass play and had a 7-3 lead at halftime. I had a feeling then that the game would be decided at the very end, and I was right. We set up the winning touchdown by throwing short. With four minutes left, we sent Clark deep. Payton found him 21 yards downfield with a clutch throw that caught the secondary by surprise. We beat Furman, 10-7 and I felt that we had beaten Nebraska. After the game, I immediately called my family to share the thrill of the victory. Led by Stephenson, the defense was outstanding, holding Tremble to only two yards per carry and giving up only 117 all night.

I couldn't ask for any more from our players. We hadn't been together long enough to know each other well, but they showed me a great deal of character. But that was only the first test. The second appeared the very next week against Georgia Southern, the defending I-AA champions. They were ranked high in the polls again. I was glad I hadn't been around the year before when Southern had buried Marshall, 63-31.

Southern used a formation we called the flexbone. It features not two or three but four quick receivers, making for a better run-pass formation. They were an experienced senior club and I realized the challenge they presented to a young team like ours. It was still warm that first weekend in October, about 77 degrees, and I looked upon it as a good omen. We had been doing all right in warm temperatures.

The second time we got the ball we scored. The execution was textbook. We went 72 yards in just eight plays, never once faced with a third down. When Hatchett went over from a yard out, I liked our chances. I didn't feel any different at halftime when the score was 7-3. If Payton hadn't fumbled, Southern might not have gotten that field goal. He lost the ball on our 18 yard line which was unfortunate. Still, our defense pushed Southern back to the 36 and I thought we were out of danger. But, of all things, on fourth down and Southern ready to punt, we had too many players on the field. The penalty gave them a first down and eventually the field goal.

Southern got its first lead after the second half kickoff. They got a 40-yard runback on the kickoff and used that as a springboard to score a touchdown that put them ahead, 10-7. We got to midfield near the end of the period but Payton's interception killed the drive. Still, we came back in the fourth quarter when we got the ball the first time on our 27. Six minutes later, we had a fourth and one on Southern's one yard line. I didn't want the tie because I felt strongly that Payton could make a yard. And if he didn't, there was still time enough for another drive. He was dropped for a yard loss and was dejected, like everyone else in Fairfield.

When he reached the sidelines, I told him to forget it and keep his head up because we're going to get another chance to win the game. Two minutes later we did. Payton made another clutch throw to Clark for 37 yards on second and long. Three plays later, Pedro went up the middle from a yard out to give us a 14-10 lead. There were just under six minutes left and it was up to the defense, which had played well all evening, to come up with one final effort. They made Southern punt after three downs, and we had the ball back with four minutes remaining. My thinking now was to run off a couple of first downs and it would seal the win. We couldn't make one. Southern got the chance they were hoping for with two minutes on the clock. They pulled off some big plays on our defense, which was tiring, and came away with a 17-14 win. That one hurt. We had played our hearts out and I felt bad for the kids. If only Southern didn't have that final drive. I was pleased with our performance but not with the loss or with something that would become a trend with our team of not being able to put the game away.

A week later I was still hurting. I had learned what it felt like to lose a heart-breaking game. Losing to East Tennessee, an 0-5 team, compounded the pain. I guess the Southern loss took a lot out of the players. Much more than I realized. They came out flat against ETSU and by the time I looked at the scoreboard, we had fallen behind, 21-0. I couldn't wait to get out of Johnson City that night. They sacked us six times in the 38-17 loss. It was a nightmare.

I also learned why coaches get gray - losing. That's what losing three straight games will do and after Tennessee- Chattanooga, I was afraid to look in the mirror. Just like the week before, we fell behind at halftime, 22-7. I had to do something. I decided that if Payton couldn't get us back into the game in the third quarter, I'd pull him and give Supsura the chance to provide us with a spark. Payton was struggling. He had thrown two interceptions and missed on over half his pass attempts, which didn't help at all. After he threw another interception with six minutes left in the third period, I yanked him. He understood.

Supsura managed to get us going. We scored twice in the last quarter, made both two-point conversion attempts and took a 23-22 lead with about three minutes to play. When Chattanooga faced a fourth and four, I thought we had it won. But we got caught for pass interference and Chattanooga drove from their 42 for the winning touchdown, 29-23. For the second straight home game, our defense couldn't hold the lead.

I had to find some answers. We were now 3-4 and faced the possibility of a losing season. That thought irked me. We had four games left and had to win three of them. The best way I felt to accomplish this was to take the ball out of Payton's hands. We expected too much from him, and, as a result, he was trying to make too many things happen. I reasoned that if we played a little more conservatively on offense, it would give our defense a better chance. In the four games remaining, two were at home and two were on the road. There was no edge there. We just had to flat out win three games.

I had to keep the players' morale up. I told them that I thought we had found ourselves in the fourth quarter last week even though we lost the game. I emphasized that although VMI had won its last two games and had the number one offense in the conference, we would beat them. We were not going to Lexington to play scared and worry about losing. By Thursday, my main concern was whom to start at quarterback, Payton or Supsura. After Supsura missed Wednesday's practice with the flu, I decided I'd be better off starting Payton.

After practice, I took Payton aside. I explained to him the new thinking on offense and he accepted it.

"We're not going to put pressure on you and ask you to do too much," I began.

"What do you mean?" he asked.

"Well, you're a good athlete and we originally felt that by giving you the ball, involving you in almost every play would make us more effective on offense. It hasn't quite worked out that way."

"I've tried as hard as I could, Coach."

"I know that and the coaching staff realizes it, too. But it put too much pressure on you and that wasn't right. After all, this is your first full season under the gun."

"What are we going to do now?"

"We're going to pull back a little. We had you throwing too many passes the last two games. Now we'll go with the run first, establish it, and throw off that."

"Sounds good to me. Do I get the start against VMI?"

"It's yours."

Before we took the field against VMI, I talked to the players in the dressing room. I needed to fire them up. "I'm not much on speeches, but I want you to listen up. I want every one of you to think about this day and remember it. Remember every second of it. Marshall football is never going to be in this situation again. Never! We're never going to have to win a football game like this to keep us out of last place in the conference or last place in anything else. I want you to remember what this feels like. I want it to make you mad, and I want you to show it. When we come back here and say our prayer after this game is over, we're going to have a lot of negative things behind us. Right here and now is where we start the road back to where you guys and where Marshall should be. But I want you to remember this feeling of having to fight to avoid something you hate. Do you hear me?"

I couldn't remember a noisier dressing room, even at Oklahoma. The players bolted through the door, their eyes wide open with emotion. Those three straight losses were far away now. I couldn't believe the numbers they put up. In the 52-7 victory over VMI, we rushed for 266 yards and passed for 249. Over five hundred yards of total offense. The score was Marshall's biggest one-sided road victory in 54 years. I was ready for the last three weeks of the season and we needed to win all of them for a shot at the playoffs.

The change in our offensive approach worked perfectly again. We were like a machine against Appalachian State, winning 50-0. There was no way we were fifty points better. We just caught them on the run and now we were. Again, we ran for more yards, 197, than we passed, 143, and Payton had another good game. In his last two starts he was 31 for 53 for 523 yards and four touchdowns.

It wouldn't be that easy against Eastern Kentucky. They were unbeaten and ranked No. 1 in Division I-AA. You can't get much better than that. The game was symbolic in that it was the last one being played in Fairfield Stadium. Maybe that would provide the players with a bit more incentive. And for three quarters of the game it did. Our defense was superb in holding them scoreless and was protecting a 12-0 lead. We scored only one touchdown and I was looking for more points in the third period.

After Pedro scored our only touchdown, Jim Bernadoni recovered a fumble on Eastern's 18-yard line. I was already counting at least three points but I wanted a touchdown. However, Pedro fumbled on a controversial call and Eastern got the ball back. That was costly. We had an opportunity to put the game away but didn't. The fumble changed everything. Yet, when you're ahead 12-0 on your home field with eight or nine minutes to play, you should win. But in all honesty, they were much more physical than we were. It made a difference in the fourth quarter when they pushed us around and got away with a 15-12 win. Again, we couldn't put them away.

The final game of the season was at Western Carolina and we brought the incentive to win with us. By finishing 6-5, we would produce Marshall's seventh consecutive winning season and I wouldn't be remembered as the coach who broke the streak if we lost. I certainly didn't want that on my record. I felt confident, but I had some anxious moments after a 7-7 first half. However, we broke loose big in the final half for 35 points and a 42-14 win. The offense, Payton in particular, played one of its best halves of the season. Payton finished 27 of 35 for 347 yards and three touchdowns as we produced 527 yards.

I had my first winning season as a head coach. More importantly, I knew we had a quarterback for the next two years.

chapter **8**▶

1991 SEASON

The Super Bowl in Tampa. A weekend of golf under a warm Florida sun. It was very tempting. I was thinking about it when Bill Parcells called me one day in late January and invited me to be with him when his New York Giants played Buffalo in Super Bowl XXV. Boy, was I tempted, but as much as I wanted to be with Bill, I couldn't justify it. Our first year we got a late start in recruiting and, as a result, lost out on some good prospects. I didn't want that to happen again, and the 1991 recruiting period was a crucial one for our program. I have always maintained that you need three years of recruiting to make your program go. Although this was our second go-around, it was truly our first full period after last year's delayed start. The Super Bowl on January 31 was too close to the February 6 signing deadline. I hated to tell Bill no. We had been friends for 19 years, since we coached together at Florida State. He had the linebackers and I had the running backs. We had hit it off right from the start and I was disappointed when he left after a year. We had similar interests and our families mixed well with one another. He was a racquetball and handball guy but he wanted to learn to play tennis. I taught him. I kidded him by telling him he was being taught by the 1965 runner-up in the ACC singles tournament. He picked it up pretty quick, too, because he was such a competitor.

I consider Bill one of the best friends I have. We stay in very close contact even during the season when we are both busy. He cares about his friends, too. He was always there when I needed him and I am always there for him, like the time he inquired about the option. And wouldn't you know it? He ran a couple of option plays two weeks later in a game. Another time he asked me about that fake field goal we used. "How'd you work that?" I told him and darn if he doesn't use it a week later. He loves challenges like that. He may be a defensive coach but he's a gambler, too.

He's been a defensive coach all his life and he's always been such a thorough one. He and I are alike in that way. Bill hasn't changed one bit from the day that I met him except he's got gray hair now. The writers in New York named him Big Tuna. Otherwise, he's the same as he's always been. He's a no-nonsense, private person, but very competitive. I'm the same way, too. I find him very genuine and special because he really cares about people. At that level, with all that success, a lot of coaches are self-centered and cocky. I miss being around him. The way our paths went in different directions, I knew it would be hard to be as close as we once were, yet we are. We used to kid each other that one day we'd hire each other.

It almost happened on a couple of occasions. In 1978 I was at Kansas State when Bill was named head coach at Air Force. It wasn't a day after he got the job that he called and asked me to join his staff. It wasn't the right move for me then, so Bill then turned to Ken Hatfield instead. After a year, Bill resigned at Air Force and Hatfield was named head coach. Later Hatfield went on to become head coach at Arkansas and Clemson.

Two years later Bill resurfaced in the pros as an assistant with New England. Then another surprise. I was with Missouri at the time and was driving around Kansas City getting ready to head for Florida on a recruiting trip when I heard on the radio that Bill had landed the job as head coach of the New York Giants. We didn't have car phones back then and although it was snowing outside, I knew I had to stop and call him. Bill's wife, Judy, answered the phone and I asked her where I could reach Bill. I knew he'd get about a hundred phone calls, and I wanted to be one of them. I had to tell him how happy I was for him.

It wasn't until the next day that we spoke. He told me that they were still playing and that the team would be in St. Louis that weekend. It was a stroke of luck. I drove over from Kansas City and visited with him on Saturday. He was all smiles. He really wanted the New York job, but he hadn't felt his chances were that good in getting it. In 1979, after he left Air Force, Bill went to work for the Giants but resigned after only two months for personal reasons.

We talked for a couple of hours and he told me that he was going to make a lot of changes on the staff next season. Bill admitted that the hardest part of his job was going to be letting coaches go. The assistants he had were all hired by Ray Perkins, whom Bill replaced near the end of the 1983 season. He couldn't make any changes at first but knew he had to before 1984. All coaches, college or pro, want their own people. Once more he reached out for me and once more I declined.

"Are you ready to come to work with me?"

"I hate to keep telling you no, but I'm not crazy about that New York life-style," I answered.

"There's some good bucks in it for you."

"I appreciate that, but it's not the money. New York doesn't appeal to me."

"I guess you're just a good ole' Southern boy."

"You're right. I'm not a city slicker."

"Well Jimbo, stay in touch."

Not many people were giving the Giants a chance against Buffalo. One reason was that the Bills had the hot hand and the other was that Jeff Hostetler had taken over for the injured Phil Simms at quarterback. I don't think anybody could have imagined what a great career Phil would have in the pros after he played at Morehead. The day the Giants drafted him the New York papers asked, "Phil Who?" But Bill's at his best when the odds are against him and he likes the underdog role. Knowing him, he'd try to control the ball and keep Buffalo's offense off the field. I wasn't worried. Bill is very perceptive and knows how to look into the future and plan ahead. He always has a back-up plan. After winning the 1986 Super Bowl, the Giants slipped a little but Parcells brought them back with a running game and a Giants trademark, a tough defense. He wanted to control the ball more and they were a lot better with the running game. If he established the run, he could beat Buffalo.

From the first moment the Giants got Hostetler, Bill liked him and was depending so much on him in the biggest game of Jeff's career. Bill felt they got a steal when they drafted Hostetler. He's always been high on him because Hostetler doesn't make mistakes. But Simms was doing such a good job, Jeff had to wait for his chance. He finally had it. Also, I remember when Parcells traded for Ottis Anderson, who many felt was washed up in St. Louis. "I just hope I can get two years out of him," he told me at the time. He felt Anderson would get him some good yards when they had to have it.

So what happened? Hostetler played an errorless game against Buffalo, Anderson was voted the game's most valuable player in the 20-19 victory, and Bill proved what a great coach he is, something I'd known all along. The Giants' defense did an outstanding job of keeping Buffalo's offense off the field. Then, when the Bills' offense took over, they controlled the ball with Anderson's runs and Hostetler's spot passing. But the key was the Giants' defense. They forced the ball inside so much on the Bills' passing game that their linebackers were able to make the plays in the open field.

Hostetler played an outstanding game, considering the pass rush he was facing. But he didn't panic and didn't turn the ball over. It was a gutty performance by Hostetler and he could have been named the game's most valuable player without any arguments. In my eyes, he was the MVP. It's ironic how the scenario played out. Bill used to tell me about Don Nehlen coming up from West Virginia University and watching practice. Bill liked Don because he seemed like his kind of guy. Now, here I am in the state which presented Hostetler to the pros coaching at Marshall.

We got a better start in recruiting. It's not my favorite aspect of coaching, but in building a new program I had to participate as much as I could. Driving with Scelfo didn't make it any more appealing, either. I swear, he could drive in the Indy

500. The first time I went with him was on a trip to Pennsylvania. We had a five o'clock appointment with a recruit and worked in the office most of the morning. About noon, I walked into Scelfo's office.

"You about ready to go, Chris?"

"Almost. Just give me a little more time to finish up and then we'll take off."

"You realize we have to meet that boy and his parents at five o'clock."

"I know. Shoot, it will take us just over four hours to get there."

"Not in weather like this. It's starting to snow already."

"Don't worry coach, I know where Pennsylvania is. Remember, I drove up there last year."

At about 12:30 I was getting nervous about travelling in the snow and making the appointment on time. I went back to Scelfo's office and told him, "We're out of here, now." We had only been on I-64 for a couple of miles when I first had to tell him to slow down. It was that way the whole trip. Amazingly, we got there five minutes ahead of time. Scelfo had a smile on his face. "See coach, I told you not to worry."

It's always an adventure when recruiting with him. We were in Pennsylvania a second time talking with a recruit and his parents in their home. The kid had narrowed his choice of schools to three, and Marshall was one of them. He was a blue chip prospect and I was talking my head off, trying to convince him that his place was at Marshall. By the time we were finished, it was eight o'clock and we hadn't eaten. The mother realized it, too, and offered us a piece of cake. It sounded good to me.

When she placed the cake on the table, I glanced at Chris. He looked as worried as I felt. The cake didn't look appetizing at all. And, when I tried to swallow my first bite, I understood why. It was the darndest thing I ever experienced. I could tell Chris was having the same problem, but all we could do was look at each other. My eyes were watering and I was trying not to cough. I downed an entire glass of milk trying to get my first few bites down. Luckily, I was able to acknowledge the mother's offer of another glass of milk by nodding. I was in agony and needed to get out of there quickly. I jumped out of my chair, looked at my watch and explained we were running late for another appointment and had to leave.

"But you didn't finish eating your cake," she insisted.

"Next time," I remarked.

There was no next time. We never got the kid. But I told Scelfo there would be no next time when it came to me eating cake. "From now on, you take the first bite and if it's good, nod your head."

Scelfo just smiled. He's always smiling. On another unforgettable recruiting trip, Chris and I were in Atlanta with Brad Lambert. I didn't have much time, just three days, so we were on the go constantly. Atlanta is a good recruiting area for us because of our TV exposure and active alumni in the area. As a matter of fact, on this particular trip we looked at eight or nine kids. It was 11:30 before we finished on our last night and we decided to stop at Denny's to get something to eat. It must have been boys' night out because there were no ladies around. I thought it was strange but was occupied with looking at the menu. But, when the waiter came over and asked for our order in a feminine voice, I realized why there were no women in the place. I don't remember who finished eating first, but I know I was the first one out the door.

On another trip to Atlanta with Scelfo, I thought we left Huntington in plenty of time to make our appointment, but just outside of Atlanta we hit heavy traffic. Scelfo starting darting in and out of lanes and gunning the engine like a race car driver. I had just reminded him to slow down again, when I happened to look at the gas gauge. The needle was on empty.

"You know what that 'E' represents, don't you?"

"Yeah, 'E' means enough."

"You better pull over and get some gas."

"For what?"

"Because I don't want to run out of gas and that's a good enough reason."

"We have plenty of gas left."

"How do you figure that?"

"You're looking at the gauge at an angle and it looks like the needle is on empty. If you look straight ahead from where I am, there's plenty of gas."

What else could I do but shake my head in disbelief. That's Scelfo. He has had me shaking my head since the first summer camp we had at Marshall. He had played with Bubby Brister, who was the quarterback of the Pittsburgh Steelers at the time, at Northeast Louisiana and had persuaded to make an appearance for a day. So what do you think happened? They overslept and I had to get our equipment manager, Woody Woodrum, to call and wake them up. When they arrived, Brister got out of the car first and started toward the mob of the kids rushing to greet him. Scelfo followed and as he walked past me with that elfish grin on his face, all I could do was shake my head.

Although we had gone 6-5 our first season, I wasn't all that happy, despite the winning record. I felt we should have won three more games. We had leads late in those games and lost them. At Oklahoma our kids were expected to win those types of games and at Marshall we had to learn how. It would take three good recruiting years to develop the type of team I wanted here. I was looking for strength, speed and depth, and we were getting there. The 1991 freshmen, Glenn Pedro, William King, Shannon Morrison, Rodney Garrett, J. D. Cyrus, plus Keenan Rhodes, a junior college transfer, all had an immediate impact on our program.

I was more comfortable with our players and I felt that our talent level had increased somewhat from the first year. We had the benefit of two recruiting years, plus some junior college players and transfers who came in. Having a good number of players returning is a positive situation. It makes for a better outlook. Some players who were starters last year would be coming off the bench for 1992. Once you start building depth, you begin building championship teams. That's why recruiting is so vital to any winning program.

We had ten starters coming back on offense, but I felt that we had more talent on defense. Almost forgotten in the five losses was the fact that we led the Southern Conference in defense in 1990, allowing only 260 yards a game. Mickey Matthews and his assistants had done a remarkable job. We now had 18 to 20 defensive players who could play and were capable of being number one unit players. Our biggest problem was to keep them happy because I don't believe in a lot of alternating.

I wasn't pleased that our opening game of the 1991 season was against Appalachian State. It was originally scheduled for later in the season but was moved up to August 31 to accommodate television. It was the first time in either my coaching or playing career where preparation time was so short in opening a season. Compounding the situation was the arrival of our family furniture from Oklahoma just ten days before the game. Since Todd and I were both busy with football, Mary was left with the burden of unpacking and settling us into our new home.

A few days later I received a phone call informing me that my father had died. I told Todd about his grandfather's death the next morning before practice and we consoled one another. As an only child, I had been extremely close to my dad and now I had to leave for two days to bury him. My dad had seen us play only a couple of times last year and his health had been failing. My biggest regret was he never had the chance to see Todd play for Marshall.

I had intentions of redshirting Todd. He had only one year of experience at quarterback in high school, but I needed him. No player had yet established himself as a backup for Payton. Cliff Scott had decided not to return and neither Chad O'Shea nor Brian Howell measured up. Despite his inexperience, Todd graded out better. I was looking for continued improvement from Payton, and with no experienced backup, I just prayed he would remain free of injuries.

We were rated in the top 20 in the preseason polls, somewhere around 14th. I felt that we were legitimate conference contenders and figured that Furman, The Citadel and Appalachian State were the teams to beat. I realized we had beaten Appy 50-0 the year before, but their seven turnovers certainly had helped. And, we can't expect it to be Christmas every game. I knew the revenge factor would be there, and I also realized I had to keep our players focused because of all the excitement about the opening of our new stadium the following week. That's what everyone was talking about, but I had to be concerned with getting our players to play up to their potential against Appy first.

Unfortunately, I didn't do a very good job. We stunk up Boone, North Carolina, and lost, 9-3. It was the worst game I had experienced as a new coach. I couldn't have asked any more from the defense. They held Appy to about 200 yards and could have easily had a shutout. I don't think their offense could have scored if we had stayed in the locker room. I was disgusted. I didn't want to open with a loss which shouldn't have happened. You can't blame the defense for a safety and you really can't blame them for the touchdown either because a breakdown on special teams had positioned it. Brian Dowler had punted for 37 yards and Appy ran it back for 37 and we got nothing out of the play.

Still, we could have won it at the end on our final drive. We got inside the 10-yard line but Payton missed on two passes and we were 0-1. The offense had let us down the entire game. There just wasn't any. We were inside their 10-yard line three times and moved inside Appy's 30-yard line five times! We didn't execute on the big downs. We didn't throw or catch a pass all day when we needed it.

I didn't like playing the game that early. With a young team, you need all the practice time you can get, and as far as I was concerned, we didn't have enough. The loss was a disappointment, but I found solace in the fact that at Oklahoma we recovered from an early loss to win the national championship. We had a chance to beat Appy at the end and didn't. That disturbed me most. We had to find a way to win games like that if we wanted to be a national champion. We had such high expectations of being a playoff team and already we had lost the first game.

Opening night at Marshall Stadium was an event I'll never forget. It was being part of something special and this was the dream I envisioned when I came here a year ago. I sold my coaches on it and the kids, too. I had a tingle when the lights were turned on and I looked across the field from the dressing room at the north side of the stadium. Oh, did I want to win tonight. Later, when I looked up and saw a record crowd, I wanted to win even more. I've never been to Broadway, but opening night couldn't be more exciting than our opening night.

New Hampshire was the special opponent chosen to inaugurate the stadium and I guess the UNH president, Dale Nitzschke, won't forget it. Nitzschke had been Marshall's president a few years earlier when plans were being made for the new stadium and was a major force in getting it built. For that, I thank him. He may never realize what the stadium has brought to Marshall football.

Unlike the Appy game, the offense showed up to battle New Hampshire. We jumped to a 10-0 lead after the first period and I was feeling pretty good. But you never know what to expect in a game. I certainly didn't expect New Hampshire to come back and score 17 points in the second quarter, all on long drives. What happened to our defense? That didn't set too well with me. Then I saw something good happen, something I liked. We came back with a long drive of our own near the end of the half to knot the score, 17-17.

Payton was having a good game. He threw a 75-yard touchdown pass to Dowler when he caught the New Hampshire defense in a switch. He then put us ahead 24-17 late in the third period with a 46-yard pass to Troy Brown on a fly pattern. But what would opening night be without dramatics? New Hampshire scored with about a minute and a half left, to pull within one point, 24-23. They went all out to win and lined up for the two-point conversion. We played pass and put pressure on the quarterback with tight coverage in the secondary. They tried a flood pattern but seeing the coverage, their quarterback had to go to his secondary receiver and missed.

After we ran out the clock I had the players do a victory lap around the stadium, encouraged by a roaring ovation. It was like a curtain call on Broadway. They deserved it, the fans, too. You could feel the excitement of the crowd the entire game. Later I found out that we drew more fans, 33,116, than West Virginia did earlier in the day in its game against Bowling Green. How was that for a history-making day? It was a tremendous win for our program. It was pivotal in the sense that we found a way to win by stopping our opponents when we had to, when it counted.

The following week, we didn't help Morehead's program. I was almost embarrassed by the final score, 71-0. By halftime it was 42-0 and I knew then that I would run the bench. No coach likes to see a score like that. We simply overmatched them and had perfect execution on both sides of the ball. Getting to play everybody was rewarding. That's what we like to do and that's why they're here, to play.

Todd got his feet wet. I put him into the game at the end of the second period after a 28-0 lead. He did all right, too. He took the offense on two long touchdown drives and finished the game with a couple of touchdown passes. "I'm proud of you," I said as I winked at him.

After a week off, we played Brown, another New England school, and from the Ivy League at that. The next time I see Joe Paterno I'm going to remind him how badly we beat his alma mater, 46-0. Paterno played there before beginning his coaching career under a real student of the game, Rip Engle, who had a long coaching career at Penn State. Engle groomed Paterno all those years to take over for him when he retired. It was a father-son coaching relationship.

The main play I remember from the Brown game is the goal line stand we made in the third quarter. We were ahead 25-0 and the defense stopped Brown four times inside the 10-yard line. That was a good sign. With a big lead, they could have easily let up enough to let Brown score. I felt that we could have a tremendous football team by the time the season ended.

Todd was beginning to establish himself as a backup for Payton, which we needed desperately. He threw another touchdown pass and experienced his first sack. When he came off the field I walked by him and saw a disgusted look on his face. "Welcome to college football, son," I remarked.

I welcomed another off-week before we played Furman, although I felt we had a peculiar schedule. After one home game, we had a week off. We then played Brown and had another week off. That's what moving the Appalachian State game did. I didn't mind the extra time for Furman. We looked upon them as the toughest team in the conference. It was a road game and a big test for our players. The game could very well determine how our football team would do the rest of the season.

Marshall had never won a football game in South Carolina. Of Marshall's 13 losses in the state, seven alone were to Furman. We had pointed to the Furman game last year and had beaten them, 10-7. Now we were pointing to them again. We started well and scored the first two touchdowns. But this was Furman and I was wary. At the half we maintained our two touchdown edge, 28-14. Troy Brown made it possible. He ran a kickoff back 94 yards for a touchdown. He continued to amaze me. It turned out to be big. Whenever you score a touchdown on special teams, it's a bonus.

I knew it wasn't going to be easy, though, especially at Furman. They got back in the game with a touchdown in the third quarter and tied it with two minutes left in the game, 35-35. I was thinking overtime until Ricardo Clark gave us a big runback on the kickoff. He made 31 yards and we were in business on our 41. We needed Payton to get us into field goal territory and he did. He connected on his first two passes and following a face mask penalty we reached the 24 yard line. On fourth down, Dewey Klein made a clutch 39-yard field goal for an exciting 38-35 win.

We got the monkey off our backs as far as winning in South Carolina was concerned. I thought Payton showed as much poise as he's ever shown. He didn't throw for yardage but his timely completions were the key. The four touchdown passes that he had were a personal high and I could see his maturing as he remained cool under pressure. The team was maturing, too. The Furman win reversed a series of late game failures, three last year and the opening loss this season to Appalachian State. Quietly, I felt that we would make the playoffs.

No sooner had the emotional aura of inaugurating a new stadium begun to fade than I was faced with similar emotional experience three weeks later. I was returning to my alma mater, North Carolina State, where I had spent my playing days and dreamed of returning as a coach. State was unbeaten, having won their first five games, and was ranked ninth in *USA Today's* poll and 11th in the AP poll. I couldn't allow my emotions to overtake me and tried to keep a low profile. One of my problems was finding about 30 tickets for relatives and friends, like Lloyd Spangler, my college teammate.

He was one of my teammates at State and we visited the night before the game. He was a hard-nosed player who never backed down from anyone. We maintained our friendship over the years and I consider him one of my closest friends. He drove down from Baltimore for the game and after dinner we sat around my room recalling our college days. It felt strange. I loved State when I played there but now I was here trying to beat them. Lloyd knew my feelings and showed his support by emphasizing that he would be rooting for me tomorrow. I appreciated his loyalty. Then he changed the subject, trying to take my mind off the game.

"How about the time John Elliott ate all those pancakes, Jim," he laughed out loud. "Remember, they had a contest at the International House of Pancakes to see who could eat the most pancakes at one sitting. Elliott ended up winning by eating 276 of those critters. Coach Edwards found out about it the next day and didn't like it at all. Remember the speech he gave the players that evening at dinner? The next day at practice I asked Elliott how he managed to eat all those pancakes. He said it was nothing. Coach never knew it, but Elliott told me that he had to go out and eat

Left
Me at 10 months old

Below
My parents,
Jim and Runette

Above
Three generations of Donnans: me, my dad and Todd

Far Right
Todd poses with me before an Oklahoma game in 1986.

Below
Coach Earle Edwards, teammate Art McMahon and I enjoyed the trip home after we had defeated Houston, 16-6, in 1967.

Left

I had spent some of the best years of my life at Oklahoma, but when the time came I knew I was ready for the challenges of a head coaching position.

Below

When we faced Morehead State in my first game at Marshall, I wasn't sure what to expect. I knew we would be an exciting team, and tradition was on our side - the Herd had only lost one game at Fairfield Stadium during the last three seasons. We continued the streak on that hot September night in 1990, by defeating Morehead, 28-14.

Above
We finished the 1990 season 6-5. It was my first winnning season as a head coach. More importantly, I realized I had found a starting quarterback in Michael Payton for the next two years.

Below
At MU Stadium's groundbreaking ceremony in the summer of 1990, I was able to witness first-hand the excitement among Herd fans and the city of Huntington for the new era in Marshall football.

Previous two pages
I will never forget the inaugural game in Marshall University Stadium. I doubt the record crowd of 33,116 will either.

Above
The crowd wanted excitement and that's exactly what the inaugural game offered. Payton connected on touchdown passes to Brian Dowler and Troy Brown en route to a 24-17 Herd lead before New Hampshire pulled to within one, 24-23, with less than two minutes left in the game. When New Hampshire tried for two, we were able to put pressure on UNH quarterback Matt Griffin and his pass to the secondary receiver missed. After we ran out the clock, I had our players run a victory lap around the field. They had earned it.

Right
We finished the 1991 regular season 8-3, and went on to defeat Western Illinois, Northern Iowa and Eastern Kentucky in the playoffs. After only two seasons, we were travelling to Statesboro, Ga., to play for the National Championship. Although we fell short, 17-25, I knew the Herd would be back.

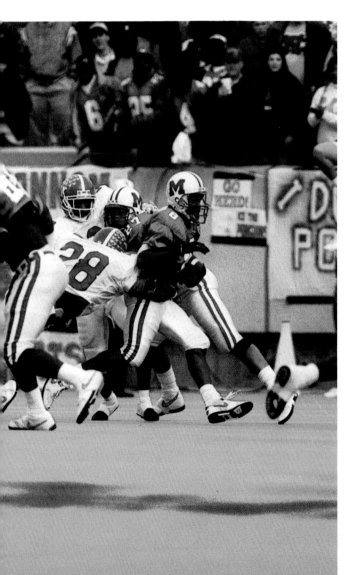

Above
When we earned the right to play for the National Championship game again in 1992, it was even more special than the year before - this time we were playing on our home turf. Each day of championship week brought a different activity, including the nationally broadcast press conference, and brought us closer to the coin toss on December 19.

Left
Wide receiver Troy Brown ended his career at Marshall with another stellar performance - 10 catches for 115 yards and a last-second interception which secured the National Championship for us.

Right
I couldn't watch as Willy Merrick attempted the 22-yard field goal. But when I heard the roar of the crowd, I knew the kick was good and we had taken the lead.

Above
After we won the Championship, everything was somewhat of a blur. I can barely remember what CBS sportscaster Jim Gray and I said to one another.

Left
It was great for us to play in front of such a large and vocal crowd of Marshall fans. After the game, the fans were so excited about the win, they flooded onto the field and tore down one of the goal posts.

Below
The fact that we had won our first National Championship was slowly beginning to sink in when I was greeted by my family: (l-r) Mary, Tammy, Paige, and Greg.

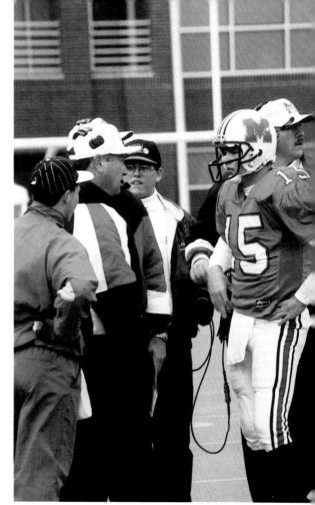

Above
I knew when we faced Georgia Southern it would be our first opportunity to show what kind of team we were going to be in 1993. We won, 13-3, and although I experienced a few tense moments, I came away even more excited about our team.

Above Right
It wasn't meant for us to win the '93 title, but nevertheless I was extremely proud of what our team had accomplished and how Todd and all the players had handled the pressures and expectations.

Right
Two times we have played N.C. State and two times we have left disappointed, but certainly not embarrassed. And the '93 contest gave me the opportunity to watch my son quarterback Marshall on the same field where I played my college ball.

Follwing page
One of the advantages of coaching the Herd is meeting so many great fans.

two hamburgers afterwards to get the sweet taste out of his mouth."

I reminded Lloyd that he wasn't too bad an eater himself. There was a place in Raleigh called Ballentine's, and every Friday night they had a deal where you could eat all the crab cakes you could manage, for one price. After the third week, Lloyd wasn't allowed back. He had given Ballentine's a beating by eating at least 16 crab cakes during each of his visits and they decided he was not someone they wanted as a customer.

When we arrived at Carter-Finley Stadium, I was reminded of the last time I had walked on that same field. My emotions were working overtime. I had begun my coaching career as a graduate assistant at State under Earl Edwards and now I was dressing in the visitor's locker room. The players knew what the game meant to me and showed it by holding State scoreless the first half. We owned a 7-0 lead, the result of Payton's 41-yard pass to Dowler in the opening minutes of the second period. I never imagined we would shut out State after the first 30 minutes and I thought this might be my day and perhaps the biggest win in Marshall history.

In the opening minutes of the third period State kicked a field goal. A breakdown on the kicking team had given State good field position on a 41-yard run back to their 44. Our defense continued to play well and when we scored on Hatchett's one-yard run with three minutes left, I felt we had it won. So did many of the 41,000 fans. A great many of them started leaving.

Then everything went crazy. State converted three third-down plays and two on fourth down, helped by two interference penalties, with exactly a minute to go, and scored. I still felt we'd win and cautioned the kickoff team of covering the on-side kick. The ball bounced perfectly for State, as the Wolfpack recovered on our 48-yard line with 56 ticks on the clock. Surely the time would tick safely away. Three straight times they passed and three straight times we defended the ball success-fully. One more down, one more incomplete pass and it will be over. And it was, or so I thought, when William King made an interception.

A flag appeared on the field and the shriek of an official's whistle sent a chill up my spine. I feared the worst, realizing that it wasn't going to be an offensive penalty. But what had the officials seen that I hadn't? They signaled a defensive infraction on Jim Bernadoni, claiming he had lined up in the neutral zone. Give me a break. He had lined up in the same spot the previous three downs and there wasn't any whistle then. How could they do this? My guys had played their guts out against a physically superior team only to get victimized by a questionable penalty that wasn't even argued for by State. Something was wrong here. I was outraged.

In another minute I couldn't see straight. State scored on a 34- yard pass play that put them in front, 15-14, with only 24 seconds remaining. We needed a miracle at that point. And they don't happen that often on a football field. At the game's end, I was livid as I ran toward the officials. Mickey Matthews was headed in the same direction. He picked up an end zone marker and slammed it to the ground, venting anger I had never seen in him before. That's all that was left, anger. What a win this would have been.

I banned the media from all the players. I would do the talking for everybody. I said it all in one sentence: "I don't care if I see this place again." The way the team was crushed by a late flag after leading for 59 minutes is beyond words. State didn't make it on fourth down but the officials gave it to them. I don't know if I could ever suffer a loss as heart-wrenching as this one. My hard-nosed I-AA team of underdogs played their guts out against my alma mater, and just as we could taste victory, it was ripped away from us. The fact that we had lost by only one point to a I-A school didn't console me. And neither did the comments made by State. Coach Dick Sheridan said his team was out-played, any way you looked at it. I agreed, but didn't feel any better. Charles Davenport, the player who caught the winning touchdown pass, was even more vocal. He said we played a good ball game and should have won it. True, but we didn't and I had to live with it.

Our situation didn't get any better the following week. We lost to Tennessee-Chattanooga, 38-31, for our second straight loss. That made our record an unattractive 4-3. It was a wild game in which 62 points were scored in the first half alone. Four of our players, Todd, Payton, linebacker Matt Downey and kicker Dave Merrick had been hospitalized on Wednesday with acute gastroenteritis, an internal disorder that causes diarrhea. It was a day-to-day situation and we had to wait until Friday to find out if they would be well enough to play.

On Friday morning they were released, but Payton never made it to the airport. Doctor's orders. I didn't say anything to the players on the way to the airport and didn't hint even to Todd that he was going to start the first game of his college career. I kept it low-key in an attempt to take some of the pressure off the situation. When I walked onto the plane, I saw Todd and simply told him that he was starting the game. I walked to the back of the plane and learned that we were down another player because cornerback Derek Grier's shoulder was still hurting and he couldn't lift his arm.

Two minutes into the game, Chattanooga rocked us with a 66-yard bomb. We managed to bounce back and even took a 14-7 lead. I could tell it was going to be one of those games where the team which scored last would win. It all happened fast. The Mocs scored the next two touchdowns and we scored a touchdown and added a field goal. They scored again and when Troy Brown did his thing and ran the kickoff back 91 yards, I thought the scoring was finished for the first half. I was mistaken. Just before the half, they booted a field goal that tied the game at 31. The Chattanooga fans loved it.

A scoreless third period gave everyone a breather, including the fans. Then, Chattanooga scored the go-ahead touchdown halfway through the final period for a 38-31 lead. We almost came back, driving to their 15-yard line. But after a sack, Todd missed on his next three passes. I couldn't believe we gave up 576 yards. We couldn't stop the run or the pass and on the plane ride back to Huntington I was searching for answers.

I knew one thing. If we were going to make it to the playoffs, we had to win our remaining four games. There was no question that we had to elevate our level of play. Before that, however, I had to restore confidence. The two straight road losses had the players down and we were going to be without Payton again for another game. On Wednesday, he was readmitted to the hospital with recurring headaches and I knew I had to start Todd again. Todd had lost nine pounds from the same intestinal disorder that hit Payton, but nevertheless had given a gutty performance in his first start against Chattanooga.

With four straight home games, we had an opportunity to get back in the playoff hunt, beginning with Western Carolina. They were a young team which improved every week and had a good sense of direction. After last week's first half which had been full of fireworks, this one was as quiet as a church service. Neither team came close to scoring. Who could figure it? From 62 points to zero. At halftime, I told the players not to worry or try and force things because the breaks would come.

The first break came on the first play of the third period. Pedro broke loose up the middle for 56 yards to Western's four. He took it in on the next play and I felt we'd go from there. But all we got was a field goal later in the period that broke a 7-7 tie. When Western tied the game in the final period, we faced overtime. I don't like ties and overtime allows a team to win. We had to have that win if we wanted to make the playoffs.

Western scored first. And that put the pressure on us, especially when we faced a fourth down on Western's seven. Todd rolled right and threw into the end zone, throwing low to avoid the chance of an interception. I held my breath as Ricardo Clark made a sensational catch. He caught the ball at his shoe tops, just inches inside the front right corner of the end zone. We were still alive.

In the second overtime, we scored first. Pedro went up the middle again, this time for 12 yards. Now the pressure was on Western. They looked at a fourth down on the 10-yard line, but we let them off the hook. They completed the pass that tied the game for the fifth time, 24-24. I started to feel that we were going to be there all day.

We needed to stop them on their next possession in the third overtime and we did. That was critical. All we had to do now was play for the field goal and not a touchdown, a big difference in determining strategy. Instead of putting the ball up, we kept it on the ground. Pedro got us eight yards on three carries and I sent in Klein for a game-winning 34-yard field goal. When he hit it, I was relieved. We hadn't played very well and we were fortunate to win. They had 99 plays to our 65. Incredible.

Nothing came easy for us. Against The Citadel, we had to rally and score twice in the final nine minutes to pull out a 37-31 victory. Payton came back and spread the field for us. He was a little weak and had trouble with the wind and threw up some ducks. However, he told me on the sidelines after an interception that he wasn't coming off the field a loser. He had a good game, going 23 of 29 for 331 yards and two touchdowns. Pedro accounted for the other three touchdowns as our record improved to 6-3. Still, I wasn't all that pleased. We weren't tackling well. If we were going to reach the playoffs we would have to do better.

VMI was our next to last home game. Like The Citadel, they, too, used the wishbone. I was beginning to think that was the war plan of all military schools. We were ranked 10th in the polls and I wasn't expecting any ambush from the Keydets who had lost five of their nine games. And, after all the close games we had been through, I was hoping for a breather. We needed to dominate a game. It would be great to beat somebody handily and provide our banged up defense some relief. Three of our linebackers, Joe Fumi, Shannon King and Donahue Stephenson, were hurting and I needed strong linebacker play to stop the wishbone.

We finally got a day in the park, 61-0. I never dreamed it would be so easy. Everybody got a chance to play and I chuckled when Todd set a school and a conference record with a 99-yard touchdown pass to Troy Brown in the third quarter. But it was Payton's day. He, too, set records. His 496 passing yards was both a school and a conference record. His 383 yards passing for a half was a new I-AA mark. We finished with 789 total yards which was awesome. Move over Oklahoma.

Against East Tennessee State, I had to be wary of over-confidence. They were 1-9. At times, pictures are better than words. Instead of talking to the players to remind them what this game meant, I put up a photograph outside the office of all the ETSU players celebrating after beating us 38-17 last year. I added an inscription: "Remember this! Don't let it happen again."

It didn't. Not even close. We hit the 60 mark for the second straight week, 63-9. We finished the regular season 8-3 on a roll with four straight wins. Going into the game we were ranked eighth and I knew a win might get us a higher rating. By winning we would participate in the playoffs. Troy Brown continued to amaze me. He reminded me of Rocket Ismail. He caught a touchdown pass, ran back a kickoff for another one and blocked a punt. He was able to do it all and I saw in him a great special teams player for the pros.

chapter **9** ▶

1991
PLAYOFFS

Payton finished strong. He set a single season I-AA passing efficiency record with a 182 rating and had our offense clicking. So was the defense which had two strong games in a row. Is it any wonder why I was feeling confident going into the playoffs against Western Illinois? I was downright excited. Our quarterback was as hot as a firecracker and our confidence level was high. I was looking for Marshall fans to pack the stadium. Maybe not as many as the inaugural game record-setting crowd, but 30,000 fans would be nice. I was disappointed when less than 17,000 came. It affected me during the pregame warm-ups and the players even looked flat.

We came out smoking, 14-0 and it was a good thing. Western was bigger than us physically and began to wear us down in the second half. The 14-0 lead dropped to 14-6, went back to 17-6 before they came up with 11 points in the fourth quarter to send the game into overtime. If we could have only booted a field goal in the second period we wouldn't be looking at overtime. We had a first down on Western's 15-yard line and went backwards before attempting a 41-yard field goal that was no good.

Western got the first opportunity to score in the overtime. They were caught holding on second down which dictated a pass. Tommy Moore was ready and came up with the interception. I was thinking field goal the whole time and kept the ball in the middle of the field by giving the ball to Pedro four straight times. We were helped by an off-sides penalty that gave us a first down on the 15-yard line. Pedro got to the 10 and after Payton lost a yard, I didn't waste any more plays. On third down I wanted Klein to win it. He did, too. His 28-yard kick was accurate and I won my first playoff game. I was excited but I didn't want to see overtime again. It's too nerve wracking.

Northern Iowa was ranked near the top of the polls, third. They were from the same conference as Western, the Gateway Conference, and had beaten them, 24-17, in the final game of the regular season. Normally that's what happens in playoff football. As you advance, the tougher your opponent becomes, upsets notwithstanding. I was hoping we would get off fast like we did against Western, only this time we wouldn't get caught in an overtime.

Brian Dowler gave us the big plays. He was basically a possession type receiver but that Saturday he exploded. The first time he came up big was on the second play of the game. He slipped away from a defender down the sidelines and went 49 yards for the opening touchdown.

"I didn't think you could run that far," I kidded him when he came off the field.

"Neither did I, coach."

"I'd like to see you do that again."

"So would I."

"Be ready, we'll call your number again."

We scored 21 points in the first quarter. Dowler scored the third touchdown and this time it was longer - 60 yards! I was really happy for him. He and Payton created the touchdown by improvising. Dowler broke off his pattern and cut to the middle. Payton saw that and gave him a lollipop. We needed that touchdown because Northern had pulled to within four points, 14-10.

"Son, how much you got left?" I asked Dowler.

"I'm pumped, coach. I'll be ready."

Just before the half, Dowler did it a third time. He pulled in a 20-yard touchdown pass that gave us a 35-13 cushion. "Brian, this is one game you'll never forget," I said to him. I was impressed by the amount of points we had scored. Northern entered the game with the country's fourth ranked defense. They hadn't given up more than 22 points in any one game and we already had 35. We pulled it back a little in the second half while the defense got stronger in what turned out to be a relatively easy 41-13 victory. Dowler finished with a career game, seven receptions for 186 yards. His father, who was a great receiver for Green Bay and the University of Colorado, had to be proud of him.

I told my players afterwards that we had answered the challenge. Northern could very well be the best team we had played. The win showed how far we had come in only two years. It was as good as we played since I've been here. It was the first time that we played all facets of the game. The key was spreading them out. If we were on and the line was blocking and the receivers were running their routes and if Payton was throwing the ball well, we were tough to blitz.

I was grateful that the I-AA committee scheduled the semifinal game in Huntington after learning that Eastern Kentucky would be the next opponent. They were rated No. 2 and were an old nemesis.

Eastern was playoff experienced. They appeared in ten of the 12 playoffs and won it all in 1979 and 1982. They were hot, on a 12 game winning streak. I was truly impressed with them. They looked like a I-A school with size and power and some war daddies on the defensive line. Their front four was excellent, big and quick, accounting for 47 sacks. I know Payton must have had a few sleepless nights after looking at the defensive films.

They executed a ball control running game with two 1,000 yard runners. I'd be happy with one, let alone two. That's heaven. They're a great twosome. They liked the ball and ran hard. They broke tackles and had quickness. That's what I saw all week looking at the films. They took a 15-yard run and made it 40. Nothing fancy. They came straight at you and we had to control their big plays.

Last year they beat us 15-12. Their physical strength wore us down in the fourth quarter. However, we were physically stronger this time. Our depth should help. We just had to wear them down some. Yet, I felt we matched up well against them. We've been tough against the run, and the way we had been playing overall, I felt pretty good about our chances. I was confident we could beat them and felt we could win it all. It was there for us to lose.

I wasn't without any worries, however. Dowler was suffering from strep throat and was laid up with a fever. We kept him out of practice until the end of the week. Still, he was weak, and I didn't know how much he could play, if he could play at all. If he couldn't go by Saturday, I would just have him punt and not line up on offense. Linebacker Matt Downey, who sat out the Northern Iowa game with a bad back, was cleared to play on Tuesday. It boiled down to a tolerance of pain and not anything damaging physically.

"I want to play Saturday, coach," he exclaimed.

"If you practice, you'll play," I simply answered.

For the third straight game we got off fast. We grabbed the kickoff and Payton took us 66 yards. He ran the last 11 himself for a touchdown and a 7-0 lead. The rest of the half was defense and we were doing the job. We limited them to 62 yards on the ground and I couldn't have been more pleased. What caught my eye was that they threw the ball nine times for 103 yards. That made me alert Mickey Matthews about being ready to play the pass more in the second half. Their personality wasn't passing but if they abandoned the running game, they might switch and try to catch us in a run defense.

Dowler was too weak to make it in the second half, and I assigned the punting duties to Mike Shoda. I was praying that the outcome of the game wouldn't be determined by a punt. The first time Shoda punted, it almost did. He shanked a nine-yarder that died on our 30. He had his head down walking off the field when I went up to him. I consoled him. "Don't worry about it. Forget what you just did. It's over with." But we got a break. Eastern was charged with a 15-yard penalty for illegal participation. Payton then proceeded to finish the drive that began on our six yard line with a 36-yard touchdown throw to Troy Brown who had crossed over the middle behind Mike Bartrum, who had drawn the coverage underneath. At 14-0, it was up to the defense to continue shutting down Eastern.

The next time Eastern got the ball, they began to throw more, just as I suspected. They scored in the opening minutes of the final period and at 14-7, it was still anybody's game. After we ran five minutes off the clock, Eastern had two more chances to catch us. They tried the pass route and threw 17 times in the 24 plays they had left. The closest they got was the 12-yard line. As the clock was ticking away, I could feel the excitement building throughout the stadium. Marshall was in the championship game and I was in coaching paradise.

Amazingly, Eastern had 25 more plays than we did but our defense made a lot of big plays, short yardage ones where we stopped first downs. In the nine times Eastern crossed the 50-yard line, they scored only once. I never thought we'd play for the championship this soon. Two years. I was proud of my staff and my players.

10►

| | | | | | | | | | | | |

1991
CHAMPIONSHIP

I became a Ray Charles fan overnight. All week long we played his recording of "Georgia On My Mind" over the speakers in our football compound. The I-AA crown was waiting in Statesboro on the campus of Georgia Southern University. And waiting for us was Youngstown State. We were seeded sixth and Youngstown 11th when the playoffs began and one of us would end up being No. 1. The music served as a vehicle to keep the players focused on Georgia and the championship. This was a new experience for everybody except linebacker Matt Downey who had played in Marshall's 1987 championship game against Northeast Louisiana in Pocatello, Idaho. In case anyone had forgotten, Scelfo was around to remind them that he coached the winners in that game. I had experienced a championship feeling before at Oklahoma and I wanted it more for the kids this time. They had worked hard from spring practice and had stuck together in the face of adversities not usually associated with a football team. Death was the underlying quotation. First my father, then Will Brown's mother and the one that we all felt, J. D. Coffman, a promising lineman who fell victim to a fatal viral infection. Death is final and no one can question its presence. We had to go on.

I was thinking about all this one night at the office after I turned off the projector. I also reflected to 1970 when Marshall's football team was tragically wiped out in a fatal plane crash on a hillside near the airport. I can relate better to that somber day now that I've been here two years. The way it's evolved over the years, blood, sweat, and tears makes it what it is - special. I wanted this championship for Marshall, above all else. To start at the bottom and go all the way to the top makes it that much more rewarding. I just didn't imagine it happening this fast.

Perhaps the adversity kept us focused all year. In a sense adversity can build character. We weren't a team of superstars but more or less a bunch of players who were focused on one thing - winning. There was still one more hand adversity played. Sayre, who played in pain all year, hurt his knee in practice and wouldn't be able to play against Youngstown. Someone had to step up, like others had all season. I was comforted by what Derek Grier's father, a minister, said earlier in the season when adversity reared its ugly head. He said, "If there's no cross, there can be no crown."

The team certainly earned their chance for a crown. They epitomized what a team should be. We didn't have 22 superstars. We had guys who worked together. There's a difference between performance and potential. This team had come as close to realizing its potential as any team I've been associated with in all the years I have coached. We made the big plays on offense. The defense bent but didn't break. Special teams were excellent. It was gratifying to come in and be this competitive this quickly.

I couldn't figure why Youngstown was rated so low. They had the same record we did, 11-3. They were a ball control team keyed by a pair of 1,000-yard rushers, Tamron Smith and Leo Hawkins. Smith carried the ball in one game 46 times! I couldn't visualize that or the 246 yards he gained. No pro runner that I can recall ever did that. Youngstown didn't have a lot of great players, but guys like Smith and Hawkins who made great plays. Wow, 46 carries! The main thing I noticed was how they played hard. Their defense was particularly impressive. They accounted for 53 turnovers that included 30 interceptions. We had to be careful with them. The way I analyzed it was, can we stop the run and can they stop our passing game?

We were leaving Huntington for the first time in two months. It felt strange making travel plans. The itinerary was to arrive in Savannah on Thursday for two days before busing to Statesboro on Saturday morning. The schedule complicated matters somewhat. The players were in the middle of preparing for final exams and the travel presented a burden. I couldn't term it adversity but rather disruptive would be a better word. We were on a roll, seven straight wins, but the biggest one was still out there. Getting Dowler back was a boost. He had lost 12 pounds in two weeks but gained six of them back. I needed him at any weight.

Some of the players enjoyed a bit of horseplay on Friday and I immediately made them put the footballs away. I didn't want to risk a freak accident and an injury that went with it. It had been a long season and I kept the practice light. I also maintained the same regimen we followed during the season, a buffet dinner, a movie and chapel service. The one hour bus ride to Statesboro was at nine the next morning. We were ready.

I couldn't ask for a nicer day, although it was a bit warm for that time of the year. Youngstown won the coin toss and decided to defer, which I welcomed. We had been having success opening the game and looked for it to continue. However, this time we went three and out. When it happened again the next time we had the ball, I was beginning to wonder. The only offense we generated the first period was a couple of first downs, and that won't get you far. It didn't get any better the second quarter. Youngstown held the ball for almost eight minutes, starting a drive the last three minutes of the opening period, which was a long time for our defense to be on the field on a warm day. They missed two field goal attempts, a 50 yarder in the first quarter and a 24 yarder at the end of their long drive.

The game was still scoreless when Payton made a mistake by throwing late down the middle. As soon as he threw it, I knew it was trouble. Youngstown intercepted and set up for business on our 38. They reached our six-yard line before settling for a 24-yard field goal and a 3-0 lead. We had a chance to tie it at the end, but Klein's 36-yard attempt sailed wide to the right. Nothing was going our way. The only positive I could get out of our first half performance was that although we played poorly offensively, we were still only behind by three points.

The first time we got the ball in the third period we scored. That was more like it. Payton got in sync and took us 49 yards in seven plays. The payoff was an eight yard toss to Brown that put us ahead, 7-3. Payton came right back on the next series, this time for 60 yards in eight plays, finishing the drive with a 10 yard throw to Clark. Here we go, I thought. After Youngstown added a field goal, we led 14-6.

We had an excellent opportunity to put the game away. Payton hooked up with Clark for a 60-yard completion to the Youngstown nine yard line. A touchdown would do it. But we got a bad break. On a third down pass that was completed to Brown, we were caught holding. I had to be satisfied with Klein's 42-yard field goal that extended our margin to 17-6. Boy, I would have loved getting a touchdown. We would have been up 21-6 entering the final period and in control.

Youngstown made two big plays following the kickoff. The first, on third and eight, went for 30 yards and the second carried 33 yards for a touchdown. We stopped the two-point conversion attempt as our lead shrunk to 17-12. Coming back, we drove to Youngstown's eight yard line where Payton got sacked for a five yard loss. It was field goal time but unfortunately no field goal. Klein missed a 30-yard attempt, this time wide to the left. I anticipated trouble. We were letting Youngstown off the hook too often and that usually comes back to haunt you.

Ten minutes remained when Youngstown got the ball back on their 20-yard line. I though we had them when they faced a third and 14. But they connected on a 22-yard pass play and a first down. Once again I thought they would turn the ball back to us. This time they were looking at third and 12. Boom, they came up with a 56-yard pass completion that had me yelling into my headset. This wasn't supposed to happen. What are they doing completing passes when they are supposed to be a run- oriented, ball-control team? Two plays later they went in front, 18-17.

With seven minutes left, time was not a deterrent. I was hoping for a time killing drive that would result in a touchdown or even a field goal to put the game away. Never got the chance. Payton was sacked, fumbled and Youngstown recovered on our 14 yard line before we could even get the chance to get going. In three plays, Youngstown scored again, kicked the extra point and I'm looking at an eight point hole, 25-17, with four minutes left. As much as I disliked overtime, I wanted it more than ever.

I felt that we'd get there when Payton hit two passes that carried us to Youngstown's 46. Then out of nowhere, Payton got sacked twice, losing 11 yards along with our momentum. I exhorted the defense to get the ball back one more time, to pull it out. They held and we still had a chance. That's all I wanted. We had a long way to go from our 17 and there was nothing else to do but pass with only a minute and a half left in our season of dreams. We had to make it happen, to move quickly against a flooded secondary, produce the tying touchdown and convert a two-point play.

Dramatically, Payton met the challenge. He was unerring on his first six passes and suddenly we were looking at the markers on Youngstown's 19. I'm thinking overtime. But as quickly as we got down field in position to threaten, we died. Two incompletions and a sack left us with a final down on the 28. Thinking they would double Brown, we sent Clark on a fly pattern down the right sideline. Youngstown dropped seven defenders into coverage but that was expected. We were just hoping Clark could shake loose. On a hurried throw, Payton's pass fell to the ground and with it our dreams of a championship.

It was disappointing beyond words. We came in to stop the run and we did. Our pass coverage just broke down at inopportune moments on third and fourth downs when drives are kept alive and eventually games are won. It's just that we had problems all year against the pass. We were better against the run. On third and long we should be able to stop the other team, but they made the big plays. I couldn't believe their passer. In the last two playoff games he threw only eight times. He passed 15 times today for 198 yards. That killed us.

As inept as we played in the first half, I still felt confident being down only 3-0. And when you're up 17-6, you should win. I know I was being hard on myself but that's what it came down to. If we could have earned an extra score at that point we would have been in good shape and the band would have been ready to play the Marshall fight song. But Klein missed two field goals he usually had no trouble making. The one that really hurt came in the fourth quarter when we were up 17-12. Minutes before we lost a touchdown when Bartrum slipped on the seven-yard line with a 37-yard pass on the way to a sure six points.

We truly missed Sayre. Payton's protection wasn't all that good. He was sacked seven times, which was far too many. We had the fans and the home green uniforms and it was all there for us. I said it was ours to lose and we did. I knew we were the better team and I knew one more thing on the way back to Huntington. We'd be back. I had outlined a three-year plan and we were one year ahead of schedule. We'd be back all right.

chapter 11▶

1992 SEASON

I'm a terrible loser. I watched films of the Youngstown game and played it over and over. It's the way that we lost that frustrated me long after the 1991 season ended. We played so poorly in the first half, the worst we played all season. I could see in the films that Payton was right. He was looking for things that weren't there. Then, the one factor in the game that I felt would be the difference, the kicking game, was the difference - the other way. That game was the only time all year that we lost the kicking game. Giving up three touchdowns in the final quarter rankled me. Ugh! A non-passing team throwing for 143 yards in that quarter alone was mind-boggling and I couldn't accept it. We had the chance to grab the moment, leading 17-6, but didn't do it. I will never forget that game.

What we had to do now was to strengthen the secondary. That was the primary need. I wasn't worried at all about our run defense. We had to work hard in the months ahead to get individual coverage from our linebackers and playing tighter coverage in the secondary. The good thing about the 1991 season was that we played better in the clutch except in that championship game. Looking at the whole 15 game season and everything that happened to us, it was remarkable we got this far.

That spoke well for the future, starting with the 1992 season. Talent-wise, we had the best collection of players we've had since I've been here. I was happy with the way our program was developing. We had a good group of kids who had now earned recognition and respect. Going through this period could only help our recruiting and motivating our young kids to do more. When people like the bus driver tell you how impressed the fans are with my team it's just like being a father to all of them. You're glad to hear somebody say something good about your kids.

We were at a stage now where the kids expected to win. Payton, Troy Brown and Phil Ratliff were All-Americans and they provided the leadership that any winning team needs. We were also lucky that we had a backup quarterback with the experience Todd gained his freshman year. Still, we had to find replacements for Madison Sayre, Ricardo Clark and Brian Dowler. One more thing. We also had to find a kicker to replace Dewey Klein. It would be a little easier this time. We received good exposure from the playoffs and even had people contacting us who had never heard of us before. Yet, you always worry about the ones you lose and the ones you've got coming back because you know so much about the one end and so little about the other.

I felt early in the spring that we could have an outstanding season. I mentioned it to the other coaches and emphasized that I wanted to make sure there wasn't any complacency just because we all had a taste of playing for the championship. What I wanted was to continue working the players hard. That was one way to avoid any complacency. On paper, the defense, even though we had work to do in the secondary, looked strong. We all agreed the offense had firepower.

Then I got an idea. We had to replace Sayre and the best way was to ask one of our senior down linemen to switch to offense. It would give us immediate help, an experienced lineman moving to the other side of the ball. Not one of them was eager to do so. I thought about it for a couple of days and figured the best chance I had to get a tackle would be in convincing Johnny McKee. The bait I dangled in front of him was food. Johnny loved to eat. Woody Woodrum, our equipment manager, told me that McKee was the biggest eater he's ever seen. McKee was my pigeon.

"Johnny, I've got something good for you," I began as he looked up from the chair in my office.

"What are we talking here, coach, hamburgers or pizzas?"

"No, no, I'm serious. But I guess you can say that's part of it. I want you to move to the offensive line and replace Sayre."

"Gee, I don't think so. I've never played offensive tackle before."

"Look, I need you. You're our best bet to cut down on the sacks we had last year. You don't want to see Michael get hurt, do you?"

"Nobody wants to see that. But offense doesn't excite me. I like to hit people."

"You like to hit those hamburgers, too. Tell you what. You can eat all you want and you won't have to worry about keeping your weight at 330 like you did before. No weight limit. How does that sound?"

"That sounds pretty good to me. All the hamburgers I want, eh?"

"That's what I said."

"Well, coach, I can't turn that down. I'll switch to offense."

"I'm glad you agreed. We're going for the championship this season and if you can keep those defensive guys off Michael's back, then we'll get there."

"You got it. Can I go now?"

"Where are you off to?"

"I'm going to eat my first hamburger as an offensive lineman before you change your mind."

To my way of thinking, it didn't matter if McKee weighed 320 or 350 because you still had to get around him. This wasn't a desperation move by any chance. Despite his size, McKee was mobile. He is one of the most mobile lineman I've ever seen at that size. He runs a 5.1 forty. He claims he can do it in 4.9 and that the only reason he was timed at 5.1 was because the field was wet. In any case, Michael now had a bodyguard.

I was looking for a big year from Mike Bartrum. He had rehabilitated one of the worst football knee injuries the doctors had ever treated. Even though he wasn't fully recovered, he showed some good signs and graded out fairly high. In 1992, he was sound. Originally, the doctors told him that it could take as long as two years and it just about did. The name of his injury even tongue-tied me. It was a structurally torn anterior cruciate knee ligament. The lateral ligament tore part of his calf muscle and stretched a nerve across the back of the knee. He worked so hard in rehabilitating his knee that we had to tell him to ease up. He was a pro type tight end. He was big and strong, a good blocker with good speed.

Bartrum was the one guy on our team that we couldn't afford to lose. He could block, he could catch, he could read coverages, he could go deep, he could make the in-between catch and he could snap for punts. He was as good an all around player that we had. He was the consummate player. Another thing. He had the best hands of anybody on the team. I figured he would play an even bigger role his senior year. I rationalized that Troy Brown will draw an awful lot of double coverage and Bartrum would be open a good part of the time. The good tight ends, like the ones I've coached, Keith Jackson, Adrian Cooper and Kellen Winslow, can make it happen on offense.

Shannon Morrison was another who had the same painful injury Bartrum had. It took him even longer to recover. A defensive back needs speed and it isn't recovered overnight. I considered him the most promising talent we had when he was recruited in 1990. I had him penciled in as a starter in our first conference game. He was also big on special teams. Those were two of the areas we needed help and Morrison was one of the best all around athletes on the squad. His ability to come back was phenomenal.

Chris Parker caught my eye during spring practice. He was a redshirt freshman who could run. At 4.5 speed, he could show you his tail lights. Yet, he had come close to losing his life in a car accident the previous spring. He was driving his girlfriend and three other members of her family back to Lynchburg, Virginia. In the middle of a rainstorm, his car skidded out of control on I-64 near Nitro. It struck a concrete abutment, flipped over and immediately burst into flames. Parker and his girlfriend's brother were the only survivors. He didn't remember the impact, only crawling on the highway away from the burning car. With those painful memories, we felt it would be best to redshirt him.

In three years even the facilities improved. The traditional media day that ushered in fall practice was the first that was held indoors in an air conditioned dining room. At least it left an impression on me. The other two media days I experienced were held outdoors in the oppressive heat of August. Even more impressive this time was the fact that I didn't have to keep chasing flies off my steak. The media appreciated it, too. I knew the first question they would ask was how good a team we were. So, I approached it with tongue in cheek.

"Look, men, I don't exactly know what to say. If I say we're not going to be any good, you'll say I'm crazy. But I can't say we're going to win every game either. We do have some players and it's nice to coach players."

That set the tone. We did get a punter to replace Dowler from Lees-McRae Junior College. Like most punters, Travis Colquitt was a bit of a flake. I don't know what it is with these kickers. He had good bloodlines though. His uncle, Craig Colquitt, was a punter for the Pittsburgh Steelers. I kidded the media about asking him any questions. He might say anything. Just remind him that our first game is September 5, when talking to him. He forgot to report yesterday. You would think with all the talk about us needing a punter he'd remember when he was supposed to come in. But Travis was a good kid. We enjoyed having him around and he's a helluva kicker.

And we had a tremendous role to maintain. Almost every preseason poll picked us to win. About seven of them rated us the No. 1 football team in the country. Who would have thought that in the third year of our program? Parcells called me and kidded me that NBC was going to do a special on us.

"Hey, every team on your schedule will be pointing right at you," he warned.

"Yeah, I'm well aware of that."

"Jim, you've been there before at Oklahoma. You can handle it."

"I know. I'm not going to react. I'm going to keep it low key."

"Tell me something."

"What?"

"Are you really that good?"

"Bill, this is the best group of kids I've had in the three years I've been here."

"I'm glad for you. Go get 'em."

"I'm really looking forward to the challenge."

"Keep in touch."

He always hung up with that expression. I didn't mind being picked No. 1. I didn't mind the fact that we had achieved that status. That's what we strive for. It's just that I didn't necessarily like being in the limelight myself. But I did like the fact that we established ourselves to the point where people respected our ability. That was a goal of mine from the beginning. I didn't mind it at all. And I didn't mind the notoriety because at this point during the building of our program we needed all the exposure we could get.

It helped from a financial standpoint of selling tickets. Nobody wants to see a loser. And, winning obviously helped us in recruiting. I remember when I was at Oklahoma, reporters from *USA Today* and the *New York Times* and publications like that used to call me. Now it was happening here. That definitely helps recruiting.

This was going to be Troy Brown's final season. I only wished he had played all four years here instead of transferring from a junior college. He did more than I imagined, a dangerous all-field player, who could return kickoffs, run back punts, block field goals and was a dynamic big play receiver. I couldn't believe my eyes when I saw his 1991 stats. He averaged 38.3 yards on kickoff returns; 14.8 yards on punt returns; 21.6 yards per reception and 122.6 all-purpose yards a game. He scored 12 touchdowns, three on kickoffs. If that wasn't enough, he blocked two field goals, a punt and an extra point in the last five games of the season. He's got to be the special teams player of the decade.

I remember when Scelfo recruited him. I sent him to Lees-McRae to look at a lineman. Remember what I said about not knowing what to expect from Scelfo? Well, I got a phone call from him that left me speechless for a moment.

"Coach, forget about that lineman, he isn't very good. I have found us a receiver instead," he hit me right away.

"What do I want with a receiver? I need a lineman to fill a hole, you know that."

"Coach, you got to believe me on this one. I got us a player you'll love."

"We don't need any receivers. What do you know about him?"

"I liked the way he walks. Not cocky, but confident."

"Like the way he walks? Chris, you've been out in the sun too much."

"Yeah, watching him work in practice. He was going against defensive backs every day that could play in the Southern Conference and he was beating them. Never took a solid hit either. He could stop on a dime and give you nine cents change. I tell ya, you're going to love him."

"How big is he?"

"Oh, 5-9, 155."

"Scelfo, I think you better get back here before you completely lose your mind."

"Just remember what I told you - you're going to love him."

Scelfo was truly excited about Brown. He talked him into coming to Huntington that summer instead of waiting for the fall. The kid didn't want to come. He had a job picking watermelons and didn't want to lose it. One day he was complaining to Scelfo that he was hot and tired. You know what Scelfo told him? "You could be pickin' watermelons in Blackville, and it's really hot in Blackville," smiled Scelfo. I owe Scelfo one for finding Brown.

When fall practice began I thought about redshirting Todd with the idea of making him the starter possibly for three years once Payton graduated. Todd had worked hard over the summer putting on 16 pounds. His arm got a bit stronger and his accuracy was better. Selfishly, I would prefer that Todd sat out a year. But I had to put the team first and make a decision as a coach, not one as a father.

There was no way I could convince myself that Payton would go through an entire season without injury. I don't think there was one coach in America who counted on going through an entire season with just one quarterback. Todd was the only back-up quarterback I had with any experience. The football decision was to play him.

As the season opener drew closer, some media members were inquisitive about how I was going to deal with the pressure of being ranked No. 1 for the 1992 season. I wasn't worried about the pressure of that at all. And I wasn't worried about the pressure of getting into a championship game. We're used to pressure. Every day there is pressure. Pressure to do this. Pressure to do that. It's all around us and there is no use in worrying about it. We still had to play the games, 15 if we were lucky. I feel nobody can put any more pressure on you than you do yourself. I expect a lot from my coaches and players, and they know that.

I anticipated a good season, a championship season. I had found a parallel between how many close games we won in 1991 and how many close ones we lost the first year. It wasn't the difference in ability, but the difference in experience. Our ability to handle adversity without cracking was important. At the same time, we had to know how to handle our success. A lot of teams reach the top and then have a tendency to find some way to decay from within. I believed that was the key for us. We had handled the adversity, now could we handle the success?

The week before the Morehead game I got together with Mickey Matthews, my defensive coordinator. I wanted to make sure we would be ready for any surprises Morehead may come up with. They were known for that. Two years ago they indicated they were going to run the wishbone and didn't. Last year we weren't sure what they were going to do. This time there was the possibility of the option. There were a lot of things we had to work on. I didn't care what Morehead did. I just wanted to be prepared for it. I asked Mickey what he had planned.

"We know they're going to be in the same kind of three-block set," explained Matthews. "It's probably some kind of wishbone or that Colorado I-bone. When they break the huddle for the first time, that's when we'll know what we're in for."

"Just be ready," I alerted him.

Not knowing exactly what Morehead would do worked to our advantage the final week of practice. It kept the players focused and they worked more diligently in their drills. Excuses are for losers and I didn't want to have any. We really didn't have any control over what Morehead would do. But I knew they were better and I wasn't looking for another 73-11 blowout.

If anybody arrived a minute late, they missed a touchdown. On the third play of the game, Hatchett turned on the burners for 68 yards. That's the way I like to start a game-fast. Before the quarter ended, Hatchett scored again, finishing a 60-yard drive with a two-yard run. David Merrick, the new kicker we got off the soccer team, showed us his leg with a 39-yard field goal to open the second period. The half ended 17-7 and Morehead didn't show us anything we weren't prepared for. I just felt we should have executed better on offense.

Outside of Hatchett's big run, we played a little sluggish. Payton wasn't sharp with a seven of 19 performance. We broke out of our lethargy in the third period when Payton hit the Brown duo, Troy and Will, for touchdowns and Merrick added another field goal. At 35-7, I cleared the bench in the final period and still came up with a couple of touchdowns. Todd connected with Ricky Carter for one and Chris Grose got the other for a 49-7 triumph.

Opening games always seem to draw the biggest criticism. I was questioned about our passing offense after Payton finished 11 for 24 for 163 yards. To me, that's pointing to the negative rather than the positive aspects of the game. I wasn't disappointed that we didn't complete more passes. We threw the ball only eight times in the second half, but we didn't need it. But our running game was better than ever and that's what made me happy. And I was happy over McKee's debut on offense. He made good run blocks and didn't tire until we ran at least 40 plays. We could see that he had to work on his pass blocking most of all. That would come in time. The fact that we were improved on our run blocking showed me that we had a better team than the year before.

How much better, I didn't know yet. Eastern Illinois didn't represent much of a threat from studying the films. They lost their running strength from the year before and appeared to be more of a passing team. They weren't too impressive in beating Austin Peay in their opener. They liked to throw and I had Brad Lambert watch a film with me studying their formations. We both agreed our secondary would be tested. But we had worked to improve it and Brad liked the progress his backs made. We were getting some cohesiveness and depth. We had worked on Eastern Illinois and Missouri, who were strong passing teams, back in the spring. You always like to play passing teams back to back, but of course it never works out that way. We rated Eastern's quarterback as the second best passer we'd see. The other was the one at Missouri.

I was beginning to expect the quick score. This time Pedro got us on the board first with a four-yard run that culminated a 72-yard drive. The touchdown drive in the second period was even longer - 86 yards, and I was pleased with that. Still, we couldn't shake Eastern. When Payton scored with only three minutes left in the half, we had a little more breathing room at 28-16. Yet, it was a strange performance by Payton. He completed 13 of 19 passes, but his three interceptions puzzled me.

When Payton avoids mistakes, he is one of the best around. He showed that by taking us on a 92-yard drive in the opening minutes of the third period and I felt better being ahead, 35-16. He then followed that with a 36-yard touchdown pass to Will Brown and when the third quarter action subsided we were in control, 42-16. At that point I was thinking that I'd get the chance to play my reserves for the second straight week.

Two plays made that possible in the fourth quarter, two plays that couldn't be drawn up and executed any better. They were playbook perfect. The first was a 63-yard run by Troy Brown on a reverse. The other was an 89-yard sprint by Chris Parker, the redshirt freshman who had caught my eye in spring practice. With that run, he caught everybody else's eye. The reserves put up another touchdown and we won, 63-28.

Troy Brown is a marvel. I'm convinced he is one of the most elusive players in the country. He's just so dangerous every time he touches the ball. It was incredible what he did that night. Brown managed 292 all-purpose yards. And it was good to see Parker break one. I was really happy for him. I've been talking about him showing people his tail lights and some people didn't believe me. Now they did.

We opened the conference schedule against VMI in Lexington. After two wins, we still weren't tested, not at 49-7 and 63-28. VMI had always played us tough early in games but we would eventually wear them down although you couldn't tell it by the final scores, 61-0 last year and 52-7 in 1990. Naturally, this brings out a fear of over-confidence. But I stressed to the players that this was a conference game and that all conference games are big.

With a wishbone attack, VMI relied on the run. It is not a good come-from-behind offense. So, if we continued our trend of getting off fast, we should be able to make VMI our third victim without too much difficulty. Yet, when I walked on the field that Saturday, I didn't know if it would happen. The field was soaking wet, but I knew it hadn't rain a drop Friday night. It was obvious that VMI had watered down the field in an effort to negate our speed.

I didn't like it either when VMI scored first. That was a big plus for them after getting blown out the last two years. They were pumped. If we hadn't scored three touchdowns in the second period, we would have been behind at the half instead of leading, 20-16. We got all three touchdowns on the ground with Pedro, Parker and Hatchett all reaching the end zone. Hatchett looked like it would be his day with 73 yards. Yet, what alarmed me was that VMI had the ball for over 21 minutes in the first half!

In the third period we had possession of the ball for over 10 minutes but never scored. We only had a single opportunity to do so but Merrick missed a 29-yard field goal try. When the fourth period began, I was thinking about how much I hated that wet field. I wasn't comfortable with only a four point lead and the field was getting muddier. They must have turned on the sprinklers all night. Finally, with just over six minutes to play, we got a big touchdown, big in the sense that VMI would need two scores in the time that was left to beat us. We went 83 yards in nine plays as Hatchett caught two 19-yard passes. When he scored on a two-yard run, we led, 27-16. The points felt good. We hadn't scored since the second quarter. We put the game away with another touchdown with about a minute left. I was glad to get out of Lexington with a 34-16 win. That field was a cow pasture and I could hear Woody Woodrum complain about how much work he had to do in cleaning the mud off everybody's shoes.

We didn't defend the pass well at all. They out-passed us, 284-254, and we weren't ready for it. Obviously, we didn't play the ball well once it was in the air. Nobody seemed to play the receiver. There was no question we had to get better on pass defense if we were going to be a championship team. The kicking game was also an area of concern. Not only did Merrick miss two field goals, but he had two extra points blocked. You're looking at eight points right there.

I was delighted with the play of Hatchett. He was off to a big season his final year and I knew I could depend on him when the schedule got tougher. In three games he had seven touchdowns averaging, was 6.1 yards a run, with two 100 yard games, and 13.8 yards receiving. He was a tad older, at 23, than the other players who affectionately referred to him as "Old Man Hatch," mainly because his receding hairline made him look older. We had a lot of good backs and I would get the most mileage by rotating them. We were a lot better running the ball than we'd ever been.

A 3-0 start maintained our No. 1 rating, which we took to Missouri after a week off. I wasn't really looking forward to the game even though I had coached there. It was a David-Goliath scenario. We were not out to prove anything. Yet, it was a challenging situation. Most of our players had never been to the Midwest and they weren't going to play a Big Eight team again. It was a once-in-a-lifetime opportunity to show that maybe they could play on a different level. Still, I wished we weren't playing the game, particularly since we were ranked No. 1. I don't want to play any more division I-A teams until we make a commitment to I-A football. Now that we have a new stadium, we could start bringing teams in here and still make money.

Even though Missouri was winless in three games, they were dangerous. They hadn't had a winning season since 1983, when I was an assistant there. I had coached there four years, from 1981 to 1984, before I left for Oklahoma. Missouri hadn't won a game in its last eight starts going back to 1991 and I was hoping they would look past us to Colorado, their next opponent in a nationally televised game that Thursday.

What concerned me primarily about Missouri was their size. Physically, they could line up and simply overwhelm us. Yet, I felt that we had comparable speed and I liked our chances to play well and be competitive. I didn't have a feel for their personnel because I hadn't been in the Big Eight for three years. But I was encouraged by what I saw on film. They didn't appear to have great speed among their linemen in the way of a pass rush, and I would be surprised if we didn't move the ball on their defense. They were big, real big, like most I-A schools. Still, we matched up with them pretty well and I felt that we could move the ball on any defense.

I had another field problem. Missouri played on Omni-Turf which was notoriously slippery, but I had two weeks to prepare for it so I looked for a solution. I called a number of coaches at Illinois, Texas A & M and Oklahoma to ask advice about the field. The guy at Illinois said it best. "Don't worry about it, Coach. No matter what you do, you're going to slip." But I did worry about it. I didn't want to be part of a Charlie Chaplin movie. I had Woody Woodrum put in a rush order for Nike Destroyers. They were rain-type shoes that prevent slipping and sliding.

When we arrived on Friday for a workout, I learned that Missouri coach Bob Stull had closed practices all week. Was he really scared? I laughed at that one. They ran every play in the history of football. What were they going to do now, run the wishbone? They had more plays than Broadway. I guess when you're 0-3 you use any psychological ploy to help your team. I wondered what the media said about their closed practices? I had experienced that before we opened the season.

There was no getting off fast this time. Missouri ran off 17 straight points with a field goal in the first period and two touchdowns in the second quarter. Pedro got our first points with a two-yard run just nine seconds before the half ended and I was glad to get on the board. Their size really bothered us. We couldn't run and managed only 97 yards while Missouri produced 259. I could tell it was going to be a long day.

Missouri scored after the second half kickoff and it was 24-7. Pedro gave us some solid running and when we scored to make it 24-14, I was hoping that maybe we could change the momentum the next time Missouri had the ball, especially after we went 79 yards on them. We tried an on-sides kick but Merrick kicked the ball out of bounds on the kickoff and Missouri got the ball on our 49 yard line. Talk about a momentum changer. They scored in six plays and went up 31-14 before adding a field goal when the quarter ended.

With the score at 41-14, I put in a new backfield. Todd opened with an 18-yard completion and Parker finished an 80-yard drive with a 39-yard run. Boy, could he run. He finished with 61 yards on just five carries and that was just about the best memory I had of the 44-21 rout. Missouri overpowered our defense. They executed 85 plays for 641 yards and I didn't care if I played another I-A school again. I had a sick feeling. This was the poorest performance by a college football team that I had ever been associated with. We acted as though we didn't have a clue about what they were doing on offense. It was terrible. I took complete responsibility as a coach that our team wasn't ready to play any better. It was a complete embarrassment to me. We might have thought that we were better than we were. We certainly didn't look like a team with championship potential.

I didn't like the extent of the loss, especially before playing Furman. The magnitude of the defeat could easily have been the basis for a downer. I had to regroup and do it fast, before a key conference game. Playing in a home environment was a help psychologically. The game itself represented a severe test in the quest for a conference championship. I couldn't look at Missouri as a barometer. They were in a different league.

There was no question that overall we had to play better. There was no getting around it. We had to play well offensively and defensively. We hadn't done that. One side or the other had been out of sync. We had to put our whole game together if we were going to go anywhere. I was encouraged by what I saw at practice on Monday. The players appeared to have put the Missouri loss behind them. We were a veteran team and it was something we could shake off. There was pride at stake here. We still had a lot to play for and it all centered around the conference and it all started with Furman. The last two times we beat them were only by a margin of three points. It reminded me of the day I took this job. About 25 people said, "Coach, you know who you've got to beat." I knew immediately it was Furman. There were over 28,000 in the stands, the second largest crowd, that must have felt the same way.

I don't know what more I could say about Troy Brown. He continued to make things happen. He brought the opening kickoff back 85 yards before I had the headset on. We were on the five-yard line and what a way to start a game. But Pedro lost three yards before coming back with a seven-yard gain. On third and one we stayed with Pedro. He was stopped and we had to be satisfied with Merrick's 18-yard field goal instead of an apparent touchdown. We got the touchdown I wanted the next time we got the ball. Pedro finished a 59-yard drive with a three-yard run and a 10-0 lead. The first two times we touched the ball we scored and Furman had to play catch up, but I wanted more.

Brown came through again. This time he went 28 yards on a reverse before he was brought down on the one. Payton then made it 17-0. Merrick should have increased it to 20-0, but missed a 22-yard field goal try. However, he came back with a 43-yarder with 20 seconds left to put us up 20-0 at the half. The defense limited Furman to only 105 yards and we were playing on both sides of the ball, something I had been searching for since the start of the season. Payton also was consistent. He completed 12 of 17 passes for 145 yards. Better still, he didn't throw an interception. Our secondary had come up with two steals and both led to touchdowns. After Furman opened the third quarter with a touchdown, Payton answered back with a 79-yard bomb to Will Brown. Then he came back with another one, this time for 38 yards to Troy Brown. Just like that, it was 34-6. On the first play of the fourth quarter, Payton did it a third time, collaborating with Bartrum for 16 yards and a 41-6 bulge. Pedro finished the scoring with a three-yard run and we shocked Furman, 48-6, their worse conference loss since 1969 and the most points they had given up since 1979. I was proud of our guys.

I was really amazed that we were able to dominate the way we did. We really got a great deal out of our defense. No question, we dominated the line of scrimmage. The kids had shown that they rededicated themselves to being the kind of team we could be. Payton was sensational, 20 of 25 for 317 yards. Our running game was there, too. Our defense forced turnovers and pressured the quarterback. It was a big win. Almost lost in the offensive explosion was Parker's 72 yards on only 10 carries. He gave us depth at running back and indeed had a future.

The Citadel was waiting for us. It wasn't quite a title game but I prepared for it as if it were. They were 6-0 and ranked fourth and we were 4-1 and rated just below them. But Western Carolina was also unbeaten and I didn't lose sight of that. We hadn't played well in Charleston through the years. My first season they beat us 21-

JIM DONNAN

10. I've got a good memory for games like that. This year I decided to practice the entire week on grass. It was the last time we would play on a natural field that season and I wanted the players to get used to the feel of grass.

I have two distinctive memories of The Citadel. In 1990 when we lost to them, we out-gained them 455-200. It's hard to imagine losing a game like that. Payton threw three interceptions and I was beginning to have my doubts about him. I decided to stick with him and go with more of a passing offense while limiting his option responsibilities. It turned out to be a sound tactical move for our team and Payton's development. Although we had beaten The Citadel 37-31 the previous year, I was not pleased. They ran for 314 yards and it was the first time we failed to contain the wishbone as their quarterback ran for 117 yards. Our preparation had been too intense. I tried to be too precise instead of allowing for more athleticism. Matthews felt that the best chance to beat The Citadel this time was to control the fullback. "If we play well enough on the perimeter, their half-backs won't beat us," he reasoned.

Six of the eleven Citadel offensive starters were fifth year seniors. That translated into experience and explained why they made few mistakes. Their line was highly underrated. Their defense fed off their offense. It's like Russian roulette trying to stop them. They could beat you with the fullback, they could beat you with the halfback and they could beat you with the quarterback. Their offense hadn't been turning the ball over and kept the ball a lot. That's why their defense played with so much confidence. They beat Arkansas, 10-3, and shutout Appalachian State, 25-0. They were good.

I would have loved a touchdown on our first drive but I had to be content with Merrick's 20 yard field goal. We broke a 3-3 tie early in the second period. Payton found Andy Bowen with a 24-yard touchdown pass and a 10-3 lead. Rodney Garrett came up with an interception to position our next one. Hatchett's three-yard run gave us a 17-3 halftime advantage, which left me confident. We had been moving the ball, producing 254 yards, while our defense had kept the wishbone in check. If we could play like this for 30 minutes more, I'd be a happy guy.

I had to wait. The Citadel took the kickoff and scored. My comfort zone was suddenly reduced. We got the touchdown back when Hatchett ran in from seven yards but later surrendered a field goal that ended the third period, 24-13. Payton then gave us a big edge with a drive that lasted almost seven minutes. On fourth and two, I went for the touchdown. It was a good gamble. If we didn't make it, they would have to go a long way to score. He got the ball to Bartrum which made it 31-13 and I could taste it. Merrick finished it off with a 32-yard field goal and Marshall had its first win against The Citadel in Charleston in six tries. It got a big monkey off our backs.

What was impressive was our running game. Pedro got 103 yards and Hatchett 99. We ran for 309 yards and finished with 507 all-purpose yards. Without any doubt, we could run the football. We had a good offensive line that came off the ball and McKee was improving every week, hamburgers and all. I didn't care what he

82 ——————————————————————— *Winning My Way*

weighed as long as he was getting the job done. Our game plan worked flawlessly. We called a lot of two-play huddles. If they were in one defense, we were going to run. If they were in another, we were going to pass. I appreciated the compliment Citadel coach Charlie Taaffe gave us. He said, "If there's a better team in I-AA football, I want to see them." We were on the way to a good year if we kept our poise and did what we were supposed to do, I reminded the players.

For some reason, it seemed to me that we could never play well against Tennessee-Chattanooga. They had defeated us three straight years, 12 out of 15 overall. The last two were particularly painful to me. They are the only Southern Conference team that I had never beaten. The game represented a critical one on our schedule. In the following two weeks, we had to play Western Carolina and Appalachian State, which meant that one of us would emerge as conference champions and earn an automatic bid to the playoffs.

Payton hadn't played much against Chattanooga, just a half game in two years. The first year I pulled him when he got rattled and last season he was bedded down with a viral infection in the hospital. I knew he'd be ready this time. He was looking forward to it. The memory of being taken out of the game as a sophomore was still fresh in his mind and he wanted to make up for it.

The defense's mission was to exert pressure on Chattanooga quarterback Kenyon Earl. The year before he had managed a career game with 15 of 26 passing for 296 yards and three touchdowns in their 38-31 victory over us. The '92 season hadn't been as kind to him. If anybody could have sued for assault, it would have been Earl. He was sacked 31 times in six games, one of the reasons Chattanooga was 2-4.

Wouldn't you know it, Payton and Troy Brown started the fireworks after we got the kickoff. This one was a 53-yard bomb less that three minutes into the game. Five minutes later they did it again, this time from seven yards out. Payton continued his hot hand with a 10-yard touchdown throw to Bartrum that opened the second period and put us ahead, 21-0. Our fourth touchdown was carefully planned at practice. Going into the game we put in a goal line run for McKee, the same way that Mike Ditka planned with William "The Refrigerator" Perry when he was coaching the Chicago Bears. On second down from the three, we called McKee's number. He rumbled into the end zone and everybody on the sideline was busting a gut laughing. But it was far from a comedy act. McKee had been an all-state running back in high school in Texas and he's tough to bring down, a runaway truck at 360 pounds or whatever.

By halftime it was 35-0 and we were easily on the way to another win. When the second half began, I put in the second team offense. We had a 52-23 win and were 6-1. The defense put the pressure on we wanted and sacked Earl seven times. He had to be shell shocked. The first half we played textbook football. I kidded McKee that he hit the hole so fast he almost missed the hand off from Payton. We really came out smoking that night. But we still had two big games ahead of us.

I would like to head a committee to build an airport in Cullowhee, North Carolina. That's the home of Western Carolina and the only way to get there is by bus. I've got nothing against Greyhound, but the bus ride from Huntington to Cullowhee is a two-day ordeal. I didn't like making the trip and neither did the players. I called it the trip of a lifetime and could easily see how the pioneers made the trip in covered wagons. As a matter of fact, after the game was over I was looking around for a Conestoga.

Since The Citadel had beaten Western 36-31, we were the only unbeaten team in the conference. The Western game and the following game against Appalachian State would determine the Southern Conference title. Marshall had never won it and that was my main objective before getting around to any talk of playoffs. Western was good, and coming off a tough five-point loss, they would be dangerous, especially at home. Cullowhee is in the middle of nowhere, 52 miles southeast of Asheville and 30 miles from Smokey Mountains National Park. I learned all that from the bus trip and I could have sworn I saw Smokey the Bear on one occasion.

Western coach Steve Hodgin couldn't say enough about us, pumping us up and trying to get our players over-confident. The quotes he made in the newspapers before the game had me believing I was back coaching Oklahoma. "I can't believe there's a better football team in I-AA than Marshall," Hodgin boasted. "That's a great football team with no weaknesses. What they've put together has taken the conference to a different level. This has to be a perfect game for us to win. Marshall is just so superior in the conference this year. I hope Jim Donnan gets the Arkansas job."

That's all he had to say to make the rumors start flying. I wasn't fooled by Hodgin's con job or by his team's 4-3 record. They came as close as anybody in the league in being similar to us from a pass-run ratio. Western had more balance than we've faced among the conference teams. Their receivers gave them big play capabilities and that's what made them dangerous. Their quarterback reminded me a lot of Payton as a sophomore, flashes of brilliant plays but then lapses of errors.

Personally, I think everybody overrates being up or down and all that. If you aren't ready to play every week when you've got a chance to win the league, then we're not doing what was needed as coaches. Where the emotion comes into effect is when you play a lesser opponent that points to one or two games and plays over its head. We were just trying to keep a steady influence on our players and make them play the same every week. That's how I approached the Western game.

With freshman cornerback Alandus Sims out, I was worried about the secondary. I told Brad Lambert not to hesitate in using Troy Brown there if we needed him. Hatchett was also hurting with frayed knee cartilage and I didn't know how much he could play. I was going to open up the offense and let Payton throw until they stopped him. After falling behind 7-0, Payton got us even with a 48-yard missile to Brown. Still, I didn't like seeing Kevin Thigpen run for 50 yards in the first period alone. When linebacker William King left the game with an injury, I became even more worried.

Seeing Western drive 70-yards for the go-ahead touchdown in the second period left me a bit edgy. Thigpen was out with an injury and Western went the air route to get the touchdown. Merrick booted a 40-yarder in the closing two minutes that brought us closer, 14-10. It was a fairly evenly played half. I was depending on getting the second half kickoff and making a statement. And Payton did. He marched us 80 yards with the payoff being a four yard pass to Bartrum and a 17-14 lead. However, when the quarter ended, Western had tied it at 17-17.

Another long Western drive, this one for 84 yards, had me pacing the sidelines when the final quarter began. A minute later I was kicking the ground. Payton threw an interception, which was returned for a touchdown, and suddenly, we were behind 31-17. I told Payton not to rush, that he was trying to make something happen too quickly. Then he took us 77 yards finishing with a 15-yard pass to Bartrum which brought us to within a touchdown, 31-24. With five minutes left, Western came up with a shocker, a 63-yard pass that gave them a 14 point lead. With wide receiver Will Brown lost for the rest of the game, our comeback would be that much harder in trying to score twice.

Payton kept throwing and hitting and leading us down the field. Then, just when it looked as if we were about to score one of the touchdowns, he threw another interception on third and four on the Western five-yard line and with it sealed our doom. The final touchdown pass to Troy Brown at the end didn't matter. We lost, 38-30, and the bus ride to Huntington was going to seem even longer now.

It was a nightmare. They threw the ball all over on us. We had been hurt that way all year. We didn't play well at all. We missed tackles in the open field and had busted coverages. We certainly didn't resemble a playoff team with that kind of performance. We put the ball in Payton's hands and he threw 67 passes, completing 36 for 429 yards and four touchdowns and we still lost. The interceptions killed us. I heard him tell a writer after the game we had played lackadaisical. Payton said it all.

We now had to play our butts off just to make the playoffs. It wasn't going to be easy, by any means. Appalachian State was a solid team despite their 4-4 record. They had four defensive players who could play for anybody in the country and would probably be consensus all-conference picks in the postseason voting. Their offense didn't take any risks and they didn't turn the ball over much. That explains why they had a conference low 12 turnovers. It's difficult to beat a team like that and our injuries made it more of a problem. Four of our starters, Will Brown, Alandus Sims, Bob Lane and William King wouldn't be able to play. Hatchett was still hobbling and I couldn't count on him. If that wasn't enough, Payton came down with the flu on Wednesday and spent the night in the hospital. I drew some strength that the Homecoming Day crowd would give us an edge, yet I went into the game worried, even though Payton would be able to play.

Ricky Carter, who replaced Brown in the Western game, and did a fine job, picked up where he left off. He pulled in a 40-yard pass from Payton for the game's first touchdown. A blocked kick left the scored at 6-0. Appy came back with a long drive, 76 yards, to take a 7-6 lead in the second quarter. Payton looked strong with a 35 yard touchdown throw to Bowen. We went for two and Payton got it with a completion to Brown. After an Appy field goal, Payton and Brown went to work. They executed a 55 yard flanker screen for a touchdown that provided us with a 21-10 lead. But we couldn't hold Appy. They scored with 30 seconds left in the half to stay close at 21-17.

Payton's third quarter interception set up Appalachian's go-ahead touchdown from 16 yards out. We couldn't do anything the rest of the quarter and went into the final period behind, 23-21. Our secondary failed again. This time a 24-yard pass gave Appy a 30-21 edge and it was getting late. Payton brought us back with his arm. In an eight play drive that consisted of all passes, he covered 87 yards, the clincher being a 31-yard touchdown to Brown, 30-28. I thought we had it won the next time we were on offense. Payton flipped to Pedro for 60 yards that put us in front, 34-30, with a little over five minutes left.

Unfortunately, Appy, which scored its first touchdown on a long drive, also scored its final touchdown on a long drive. We couldn't stop them. They went 72 yards, with the game winner being a nine yard pass with eight seconds remaining that left us with our heads down, 37-34. It was the first loss in our new stadium in 15 games. We were 6-3 now, having lost two straight and seriously damaging our playoff chances. I was dejected. Before we played another game, we had to regroup and regroup fast. I had never expected this.

Before our last home game of the regular season against Tennessee Tech, I told the squad about picking it up and making the plays needed to win games. We hadn't been doing that. I reminded them of what Hatchett did for us against Appalachian State. He was hobbling when I sent him into the game with nine minutes left - on a fourth and two. I had enough faith in Hatchett's determination to make the first down. He caught a screen pass and turned it into an 11-yard gain that set up a touchdown on the next play. The sight of Hatchett picking himself up and limping off the field was inspiring, one that I impressed upon the players.

I was perplexed by the drop off defensively. I consulted with Matthews about it, looking for a solution. We appeared to be playing on our heels, waiting, instead of attacking. I told Matthews that I wanted his unit to be aggressive and play with reckless abandon. Then I reminded Lambert that although the secondary was not giving up the big play, we were giving up too much in front. We were not the team we were two weeks ago. Our confidence level slipped and I was scared of Tennessee Tech.

They were a hot team on a six-game winning streak. At 7-2, they had a better record than we did. When a team wins six games in a row, it can play with a lot of confidence. Their defense was the best in the Ohio Valley Conference, averaging 283 yards a game. I really appreciated what Tech coach Jim Ragland had noticed about our program and I hoped every Marshall graduate read what he said: "The thing I'm happy about for Marshall is that when I was at WVU, Marshall was looked upon as the stepchild in West Virginia," he was quoted. "They didn't get the respect they deserved. Marshall's done a good job upgrading the program. It's first class. I'm very impressed with what they've done with their backing and their crowds. They're committed to having an excellent program."

We didn't draw well for our final home game. Only about 15,000 showed up. We had to show that we were still a playoff caliber football team. If the first quarter was a barometer, we were marking the gauges. We scored three touchdowns for a 21-0 lead before Tech could catch its breath. Bartrum caught a five-yard touchdown pass, Pedro ran for a four-yard score and McKee excited the fans from one yard out. The 21-point bulge remained at halftime.

Then McKee did his number again and Troy Brown caught a 10-yard pass in the end zone from Payton and at 35-14, we looked as if we were getting back to where we were before losing two straight games. Special teams were also back. Brown blocked a punt that Tony Williams picked up and ran for a touchdown. That, added to Merrick's field goal, gave us a 45-14 advantage after three periods. Todd got us the final touchdown in the fourth period with an 11-yard pass to Ricky Carter for a 52-14 triumph.

That was more like it. We played a complete game, offensively and defensively. The defense controlled Tech and the offense had Tech on its heels. We looked efficient again. When we play with intensity, nobody can stop us, which was what I told the players afterwards. We could see it by analyzing the statistics: 25 first downs to eight; 77 plays to 59; and 483 yards to 212. It was a complete game, all right. I felt this effort was the one to turn things around and save our season.

The way the players were thinking, the Tennessee Tech game was the beginning of the playoffs. Their analogy was correct. We had to win that game and the final one at East Tennessee State to finish 8-3 and wait for a playoff bid. State was 5-5 but our players were focused. They looked at State not as a team that lost five games but one that stood in the way of the playoffs. That attitude prevailed during practice and was evident when the game began.

We served notice by scoring three touchdowns in the opening period: Bartrum caught a six-yard pass, Brown grabbed one for nine and Hatchett, who was healthy again, ran the third one in from two yards out. We had a good mix on offense. In the second quarter, Payton continued to look sharp. He completed three straight passes to set up Brown's eight-yard touchdown reverse and capped the first half with a nine-yard touchdown strike to Bartrum. With the score 35-3, there was no doubt about the outcome. Two more touchdowns in the second half gave us an easy 49-10 win and a complete performance we hoped would impress the playoff committee which would be announcing the 16-team playoff field the next day. We finished 8-3 overall and second in the Southern Conference with a 5-2 record.

chapter 12▶

1992
PLAYOFFS

I was watching the Denver Broncos-Los Angeles Raiders game on television late Sunday afternoon when I received a phone call from Lee Moon telling me that Eastern Kentucky would be our opening playoff opponent. I was thrilled we were included in the 16-team field. I looked at our games against Eastern like the games between the Broncos and Raiders, a heated rivalry. Their program was as advanced as ours, truly one of the finest in I-AA, and we had been playing them on a home and home basis. However, the rivalry subsided in 1990 when scheduling difficulties forced us to drop them from the schedule.

Eastern finished the season 9-2 and was ranked 12th. We closed at 8-3 and were rated sixth. That bothered Eastern's coach Roy Kidd. He couldn't understand why we were ranked ahead of him. He claimed his two losses were to ranked teams and we had two losses to inferior teams and because of that Eastern should have been ranked higher. I couldn't care about ranking at this point. We were in the playoffs, and if we kept on winning, the No. 1 ranking was all that mattered at the end.

This was supposed to be somewhat of a rebuilding year for Eastern. They had a couple of decisive losses to Samford, 46-14, and Middle Tennessee, 38-7. But if 9-2 is a down year, I'll take it any time. I was even more impressed by the fact that Eastern was making its seventh consecutive playoff appearance and a record 13th appearance in the 15 years I-AA playoffs had existed. That speaks a ton for the program Eastern had going. We had beaten them 14-7 in last year's semi-final, but this year we were a better offensive team and I'd be surprised if we didn't score more.

I felt more confident about our team than at any other time this season because of the way we were playing and the health of the players. Linebacker William King showed what a force he was with the defense. We also got defensive end Bob Lane and cornerback Alandus Sims back from mid-season injuries. Hatchett's appearance in the offensive lineup gave us more versatility, and I was pleased with the way we had played in the final two games. But we had to stop Eastern's running back Markus Thomas. He had run for an unimaginable 300 yards against us two years before and was now the leading rusher in I-AA history. In 1991's playoff game against EKU, we held him to 57 yards and that was the reason we won. Our game plan was the same. Go after Markus and make them throw the ball. I was hoping that if we could force them into some lost yardage plays, they would lose confidence in the running game.

Tackle Jim Durning was one of the first to make a statement. On the second play of the game, he dropped Thomas for a five-yard loss. That was what I was looking for. It left Thomas thinking. Eastern went three and out and set the tone for the defense. We didn't hesitate in scoring. Hatchett make it into the endzone with a two-yard run. Then Merrick added a 34-yard field goal for a 10-0 lead.

The game was over by halftime, which I never expected. We exploded for 24 points and a 34-0 lead. I enjoyed watching the offense execute. First Troy Brown caught a 37-yard touchdown pass. Then he brought the crowd to its feet with a 71-yard punt return for a 24-0 lead. I sensed that this was our day. The return was a back breaker and Eastern walked off the field with its head down. McKee made his one-yard rumble and Merrick booted a 33-yard field goal and there was no way Eastern would catch us.

It was kind of unbelievable the way we played in the first half. We put it all together. Our defense had set the table with a lot of lost yardage plays. They controlled the ball the second half, too. They continued to frustrate Thomas and we finished with 10 more points, the first being a 44-yard Payton to Brown touchdown pass in the third period. Then Merrick closed shop in the fourth period with a 24-yard field goal for a 44-0 final.

I didn't have any doubt that we would play well but this was too good to be true. I didn't think we'd dominate, but that's something you can't predict. I enjoyed it while I could. The defensive front had been good against the run against every team we played, just like today. That was the real strength of our team. They held Thomas to -4 yards and Eastern to 192 overall. No coach could ask for more than that. Or for more than the 524 yards the offense produced. Payton was outstanding with 26 of 35 passing for 353 yards and two touchdowns. What I liked best was that he wasn't sacked and didn't throw an interception. And, oh, that Troy Brown with 287 all-purpose yards. I was wondering if it could get any better than this.

Mickey Matthews came into my office after watching films of our second round opponent, Middle Tennessee State. He was shaking his head.

"What do you have?" I asked him.

"Coach, we got us a tiger by the tail."

"How big?"

"Plenty big."

"In what way?"

"This is the best offensive team we've played in three years."

"Are you serious? That's saying a lot."

"I know. I don't know if they are the best but they are the most explosive."

"Let's have a look."

Mickey was right. Middle had three speedy backs who had gained over 500 yards each. It may not sound like much. But when you look at it cumulatively, that's an impressive amount. What caught my eye was their offensive line anchored by Steve McAdoo, a two-time Kodak All-American. At 6-4, 282 pounds, he was definitely NFL size. The line excelled in run blocking and he was the main reason. They weren't great pass blockers but to get to their tailbacks, we had to get off their blocks quickly.

I expected their secondary to play man coverage. I was hoping that we would eventually face such a defense because our receivers had the quickness to get open in one-on-one coverage. All season we went up against the zone. Middle used a 50 defense in which they would drop a linebacker into coverage. They were that fast, probably the fastest team speed that we went up against all year. The other defensive alignment that they depended on was the wide tackle six which allows them to rush the passer.

Middle was 10-2. One of their losses was to Nebraska, 48-7, a Big Eight powerhouse. The other was to Georgia Southern, 13-10. They weren't as big as we were and I was hoping the 40 pound per man advantage of our offensive line would give us the pass protection we needed. Their speed and quickness were obvious. They were the Oklahoma of I-AA and I felt this game was for the national championship. I wasn't putting down any of the remaining playoff teams. It was just that I believed Middle was that good.

Cold weather discouraged the crowd. Only 14,000 showed up for the Eastern Kentucky game, which was 2,000 less than the week before. I was encouraged by what we did after Brown returned the opening kickoff 36 yards to the 42. Payton took us the rest of the way and scored the touchdown with a six-yard run. I didn't have much time to enjoy it. On our third series, Payton was hammered for a five-yard loss and rolled over in pain holding his knee. I didn't know it then, but he was gone for the day.

A defensive breakdown got Middle back into the game as Brigham Lyons ran 81 yards for a touchdown. Nobody should run 81 yards with a football and it just about killed me. With Payton out, I turned to Todd. I took him aside and told him to relax, that we weren't going to do anything fancy and not to try to do too much by himself. Just play the way you did all year and look at it as the thirteenth game of the season.

By the second quarter, Todd had relaxed and showed it with a 42-yard completion on which Brown made a sensational catch. The play got us moving.

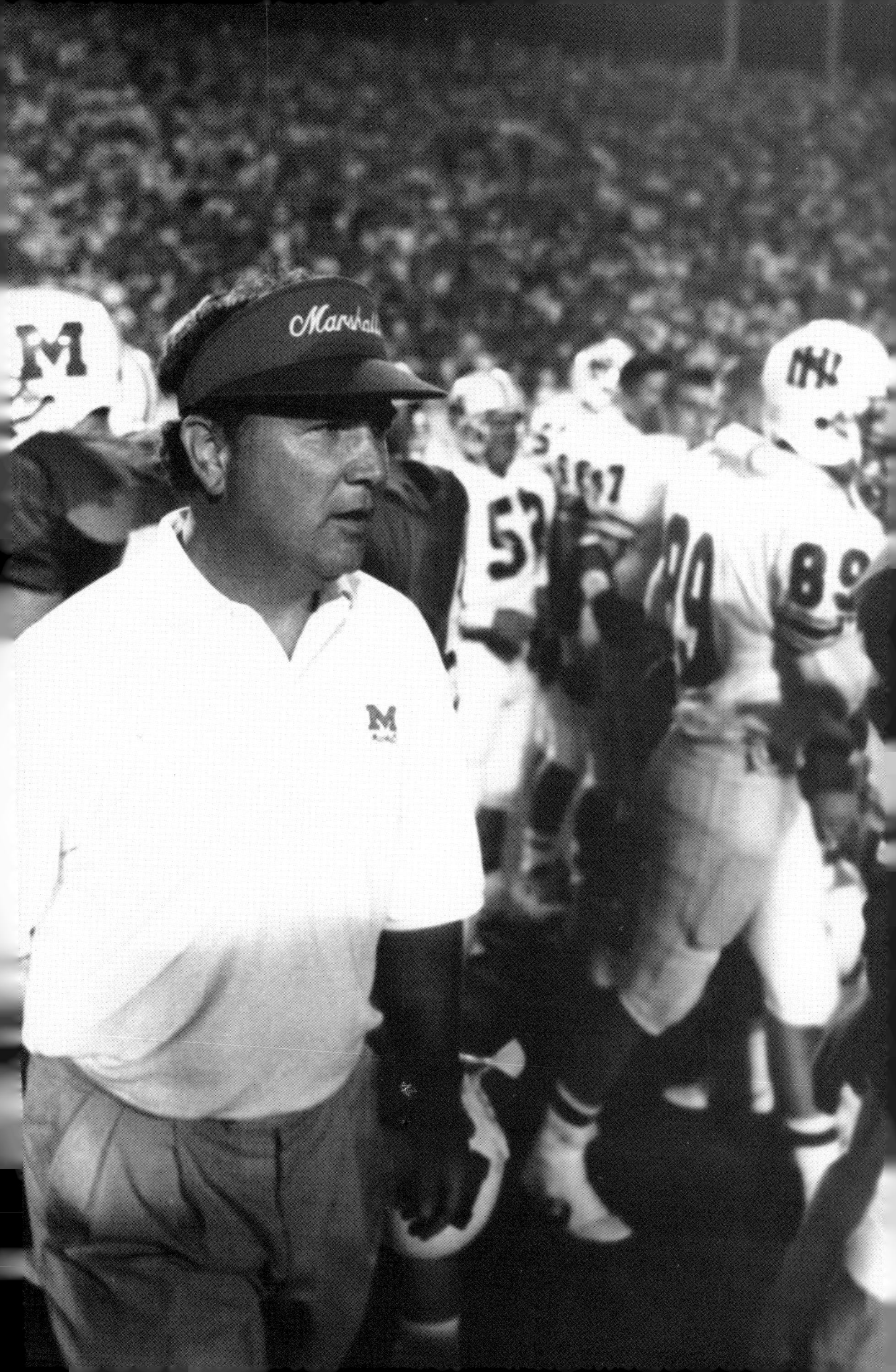
Marshall
M
57
89
89

Above Talking with Roman Gabriel before The Citadel game in 1993.

When Pedro scored from three yards out eight plays later, we regained the lead, 14-7. Todd and Brown hooked up for another big completion, this one for 45 yards and a touchdown. Leaving the field at halftime with a 21-7 lead gave us momentum. I learned from our trainer, Jamie Perez, that Payton wouldn't be able to finish the game. It was now up to Todd and the rest of the team to get the job done. Middle had been successful running the ball 161 yards, but I knew being behind two touchdowns, they would have to put the ball up in the second half.

Todd came through again. The first time we had possession in the third period he amazed me. We were in negative field position on the two-yard line. A turnover there and Middle would score, get back into the game and probably swing the momentum to their side. I put Todd on the spot. If he was going to grow as a quarterback, it would be now. He responded more than I imagined. First, he completed a 25-yard pass to Brown to get us out of the hole. Next, he threw a 24-yarder to Ricky Carter, and just like that we had a drive going. Then he hit Pedro out of the backfield for five yards. After Pedro lost three yards, Todd came back with another long gainer, 34 yards to Brown. He wasn't finished yet. He made me the proudest father in the world with a 13-yard touchdown pass to Brown for a 28-7 advantage. Todd did the impossible, taking us 98 yards. If I had had a house phone, I would have called Mary in the stands. That's how happy I was.

I wasn't even upset when Middle scored to open the fourth quarter. Todd appeared in control. However, a few minutes later, I had to caution him after he forced an interception. "Look, I know you're pumped and you're going good, but take it slow," I advised him. He settled down, so much so, that he took us on an 80-yard drive that clinched it. The payoff was a five-yard pass to Brown. The game ended in our favor, 35-21, and we were in the semi-finals as Todd finished 13 of 23 for 246 yards and three touchdowns. His mother was waiting to hug him.

Almost lost in the excitement was Pedro's 119 rushing yards and another blue ribbon day by Brown. I thought then that if some pro team didn't draft him, I was crazy. He produced 264 all-purpose yards and had managed one catch by out-jumping two defenders that was highlight film material. Todd's performance substantiated my decision in September not to redshirt him. We would have been in dire straits. I had a word with him privately.

"Son, I was real proud of you out there."

"Thanks, Dad."

"You responded in a pressure situation and grew up today. This is what football is all about."

"You always taught me about challenge and I wanted to give the seniors another chance to play."

"They'll appreciate what you've done."

"I went out and played the best I could because this team can go a long way."

I would have been happy with the '92 season even if it had ended that day. I was on a high. In the semi-finals we were paired against a tough Delaware team that was 11-2. They reached the semis by destroying Northeast Louisiana, 41-18, the week before in Monroe, Louisiana. It was quite an accomplishment when realizing that Northeast was rated No. 1 at the time.

On Monday night I learned that Payton had not suffered a torn ligament but instead had cartilage damage. Nothing severe, though. He would be able to play Saturday and that was a relief. I really needed him. Hatchett, who sustained a concussion, was doubtful. He was still light-headed and his status would remain questionable until the latter part of the week. I had already made my mind up that if he couldn't play, I would make Pedro the hot runner. I gave Todd a lot of snaps in practice just in case Payton, who was in a leg brace, experienced problems planting his foot.

I had always maintained that throughout the season our run defense was exceptional. It would have to be that and more against Delaware. Their Wing-T emphasizes the run and Delaware maximized its meaning. They had 3,590 yards rushing which enabled them to keep the ball 63 minutes more than their opposition. That's a full game. Their quarterback, Bill Vergantino, was intelligent, quick and diverse in utilizing his running and passing skills. Delaware featured a 1,000-yard runner in Daryl Brown, but Vergantino was right on his heels with 822 yards. With Delaware averaging 276 yards rushing, our run defense was facing a challenge.

Delaware used a lot of mis-direction and quick-hitting type plays in their offense. The trick was not to over-react but to wait a split-second and read. They had guards pulling one way and backs going the other way, trying to create confusion. They used a lot of motion prior to the snap and the secret was not to get mixed up in all of that movement but to wait a split-second after the ball is snapped and then react to the ball.

Delaware had extreme confidence in its offense. Maybe too much. Their quarterback was a bit outspoken, a trait I don't tolerate among my players. "We've been able to move the ball on everyone we've faced in the playoffs," Vergantino said. "Marshall shouldn't be any different. They look just like another 4-3 to me." That's bulletin board stuff. Their coach, Tubby Raymond, offered more. "We shouldn't have any trouble running the ball on the ground against Marshall," he added. "We've been able to move the ball on the ground against anybody." They must have been reading from the same script.

Payton could play but Hatchett couldn't. With Payton's limited mobility, we didn't want him trying to scramble around. I started Parker in Hatchett's spot but depended on Pedro to do the bulk of the running. We started the game with three running plays to allow Payton to get used to his knee brace and were forced to punt after gaining only eight yards. Delaware's offensive personality wasn't a surprise; they ran. They passed only once in an 11-play, 59-yard drive that got them a touchdown.

On our second series, we went the other way. Payton tried three passes and we fizzled again. He completed one, threw an incomplete pass and was sacked. It wasn't pretty, but that wasn't even the worst part. It was Travis Colquitt's 13-yard punt. Delaware got the ball on our 37. This wasn't a good way to start a game, playoffs or not. Four rushing plays carried Delaware to a first down on the 14-yard line. Then they deviated from what had been working for them and tried for a quick touchdown. After an incomplete pass, they went back to the run and lost three yards. On third down, Shannon Morrison stopped their momentum with an interception at the four-yard line.

We played poorly in the first period. We didn't make a first down and hadn't shown that we could stop Delaware who scored, threatened two other times and made seven first downs. They turned the ball over twice, the last time with a fumble on our 31, otherwise they might have scored more points. Midway through the second quarter we came to life. Payton completed four consecutive passes in a 51-yard drive that tied the game, 7-7. McKee charged up the crowd by barreling in from the one-yard line and I was a lot more confident.

At halftime, we kept the adjustments Matthews made on defense after the first period. We turned Keenan Rhodes and Jim Durning loose on the line and sent Shannon King up the middle. This made it difficult for them to pull their guards. They didn't make a first down the entire second quarter and we decided to stay with it. Yet, in the third period, Delaware threatened again. They got as far as our 28-yard line but missed a 45-yard field goal attempt.

It didn't look promising when Payton took an eight-yard sack on our 20. But when Pedro got 13 and Payton ran for 12, we got on track. We took the lead for the first time on a perfectly executed screen pass to Pedro. However, we still had another quarter to play and I wasn't too comfortable with only a 14-7 lead. Then, when Vergantino became ill and was replaced by Delaware's leading passer, Dale Fry, I thought that they would probably try to put the ball in the air more. It didn't matter.

In the fourth quarter we assumed control as Payton led us on a 14-play, 78-yard drive that consumed seven minutes. He scored on a four-yard run that gave us a 21-7 edge. Minutes later, the defense responded. Roger Johnson picked off a pass and excited the crowd with a 79-yard touchdown run that sealed a 28-7 victory. Our defense was magnificent after the first series when Delaware scored. We had a tough time getting our offense going, but after the second quarter we took control of the line of scrimmage. Still, it was the first time I had ever experienced going through an entire quarter without a first down. I was a little embarrassed by it.

The embarrassment was shoved aside after the game, though, when I was doused with a bucket of Gatorade. I looked around for the perpetrator. It was Todd.

||||||||||||

chapter 13

1992
CHAMPIONSHIP

I t was eerie. Somehow, everything seemed to flash back to 1970. Payton was only seven months old when the Marshall plane crash wiped out the football program. I learned about the tragedy when I got here. It's something that comes with the school. The thoughts and emotions of fans were expressed throughout the city: this is for the victims of the crash; this is for the entire town and the community. Those sentiments were on our minds every day of practice. It was as if the players were on a mission.

Our entire season had come down to Youngstown State. I thought it was fitting for us to be facing Youngstown again; we had another chance at the National Championship against the team which had snatched it from us the year before. The 1992 I-AA championship game would be a rematch of the 25-17 heartbreaker of 1991. Only this time, instead of Statesboro, Georgia, we were to meet in Huntington where we were 17-1 and there were 31,000 fans waiting to yell "Go, Herd!" At the beginning of the week I dismissed immediately the thoughts of revenge from the minds of the players. I didn't want them to get caught up in the melodrama. I emphasized that we were playing for a championship ring. That was primary. Win the game, get the ring and take whatever else you want afterward.

More than anything else, our kicking game had led to 1991's downfall. We missed two field goals and they kicked two. They ran a kickoff back and Troy Brown never touched the ball in a kicking situation. Brian Dowler averaged only 13.5 yards on two punts in windy conditions. It couldn't have been any worse than that. Obviously, we had to do a better job on special teams than we did last year. There wouldn't be any surprises, either. Youngstown knew us and we knew them. They came straight at you with one of the country's strongest running attacks.

They did so with two 1,000-yard runners, Tamron Smith and Darnell Clark, who had the comfort of running out of the I-formation behind a line that averaged 283 pounds. Is this the NFL or what? It was no surprise that they ran straight ahead with that kind of beef. They also created another problem with a 1,200-yard receiver. We had our hands full. It wasn't going to be easy getting that ring and it boiled down to which team would execute better. They were bigger and we had to rely on our quickness. We hadn't played anybody as big and strong as they were, but we were ready to play and I am sure they were, too. And, I was thankful that Hatchett was able to join us.

David Merrick wasn't. He had missed practice on Thursday and had no excuse. I called my staff together for a discussion about a player who had broken a team rule that automatically called for a suspension. Do we put the magnitude of the game before the rule and let him play, or do we uphold the penalty? The staff unanimously concurred that if a rule was violated, then it must be enforced. I had no choice but to suspend Merrick.

Now we were faced with a problem I hadn't expected to hit us 48 hours before a championship game. We had to find a kicker. We looked to David's older brother, Willy, who had kicked off for us a couple of times and was the leading scorer on the Marshall soccer team, but never had attempted a field goal. He wasn't receptive to the idea of replacing his brother. His loyalty to him was natural. But after explaining how important it was and how desperately we needed him, he relented and agreed to kick. I could only hope that the game wouldn't come down to a pressure field goal.

If I was ever a prime candidate for an ulcer, it would have been now. I had a week of disruption that I would never forget and it wasn't all final exams, either. Payton missed a day of practice. He was in New York receiving an award as the I-AA Player of the Year. Troy Brown was in the hospital overnight with strep throat, and I had a green kicker who had never kicked a field goal in his entire life. I only hoped that he could, if the game was on the line.

Also, I was hoping that we would win the coin toss. We did. I wanted to start the game on offense. Still, we didn't score in the first quarter and neither did Youngstown. However, we moved the ball both times we had it and I was encouraged. When the second period opened, we broke through with an 80-yard drive. Payton finished it with a six-yard pass to Bartrum on a fourth and goal. Near the end of the half, we scored again on a turnover after Shannon Morrison put us in business by recovering a fumble on Youngstown's 28-yard line. Seven plays later, Hatchett bounced in from the five and we had a 14-0 halftime lead. The defense was playing big time. They held Youngstown to just three first downs and 66 total yards. I wasn't hyperventilating just yet. I knew a win wouldn't be that easy and there was last year's game to remind me.

Youngstown received the second half kickoff and our defense continued to stop them. Three and out and we took over on our 22-yard line. Just like a Timex, the offense kept ticking. They went 78 yards in nine plays with Pedro carrying it in from one yard out for a 21-0 advantage. Five minutes later, cornerback George Thomas intercepted a pass on our 26-yard line and ran it back 52 yards to the Youngstown 22 to set up our fourth touchdown. On the next play, Payton got it to Hatchett with a screen pass to push our edge to 28-0 at the 5:36 mark. I couldn't believe what was happening. Could it really be this easy?

I got the answer soon enough. Two big passing plays accounted for Youngstown touchdowns just when it looked as if they were finished. The first was a 30-yard touchdown pass and the other was a 42-yarder to our one-yard line. They ran it in from there and suddenly it was 28-14. As I thought at the half, it wouldn't be easy. Scoring two touchdowns in five minutes concerned me. It brought back visions of 1991 when we blew our 11-point lead. I was beginning to miss William King out there on defense. He had been taken to the hospital in the third quarter with a neck injury, and I knew he wouldn't be back to help.

Again Youngstown scored. In the opening minutes of the fourth quarter they went 49 yards in only four plays, beginning with a 34-yard pass completion. It was another big play and another touchdown. What's going on here? Their last three possessions Youngstown had scored. I was experiencing déjà vu. It was 28-21 with ten minutes left. I felt a bit relieved when we stopped them the next time they had the ball. However, we couldn't generate any offense and Youngstown got the ball back with about six minutes left. They were on their 11-yard line and 89 yards looked like a mile. However, it didn't faze Youngstown. They went the entire distance for the game-tying touchdown and with 2:23 flashing on the clock, it was 28-28. Not again. We had to win it this time.

I told Payton that a field goal would do it. I instructed him not to try and get us in field position all at once, just play his game and take what they'd give us. The mission was the Youngstown 25-yard line. After the kickoff, we were set on the 19 and Payton looked poised and confident as we began our drive to destiny. His first test was a third and one on the 39 and he responded by running for two and a first down. Moments later, he looked at a third and four at the Youngstown 40. A five-yard pass to Pedro kept us alive. Once again he was challenged. On a second and eight on the 33, he completed a 14-yard pass to Troy Brown at the 19.

We had the field goal yardage, but I wanted to make it easier for Willy. Two straight ahead runs would do it. Payton got six and Hatchett eight and the ball was in the middle of the five-yard line. It was time for Merrick. Tim Billings had his arms around him during the time out. He told him not to look at the clock, not to think about the score, but to concentrate on the goal posts and kick it the way he did in practice.

That's all there was to it. Yeah, sure. A field goal. Why did the game have to come down to this? Youngstown then called a time out with ten seconds left, to let Merrick think about it. We reminded Willy to think about the goal posts 22 yards away. I began worrying about the snap and the placement and the follow-through on his kick. The worst fear I had was a block. I put my head down. I couldn't look. I'd let the Marshall crowd of 31,000 let me know what happened. The wait seemed like an eternity. Then I heard a tumultuous roar. It was the most electrifying crowd noise I had ever heard and I knew what it meant. Willy had done it. Willy the soccer player. Willy the hero. Marshall had won the first football championship in its history. I didn't know who to grab first. It had to be Willy.

I had hoped that the game wouldn't come down to a pressure kick, but it had. It was bizarre. Willy's brother, David, was on the sidelines the entire game and it should have been his kick, his game to win. What could have been more dramatic than this? No one in Hollywood could have written a more dramatic ending. And the ending went beyond the field. The championship was for the community, for Huntington, for those who were killed in that unforgettable plane crash in 1970 that left open wounds on hundreds of lives. The championship helped heal those wounds though the memories will remain. Hatchett put it in perspective.

"Destiny just took charge today," he began. "The man upstairs had a great feeling. He kept us strong because it was a long, hard game. But He just kept us going and we kept the spirit up. The spirit that was in the stadium today was incredible. You could feel the people who gave their lives and the people who sweated and bled for this Herd team. It all came together. The spirit that filled this stadium today helped Marshall to win a championship. That's what makes our fans so sincere. They're not just jumping on the bandwagon. I think this really makes Huntington a close-knit community. And I think we still feel the pain of the losses even after two decades. I hope that today eases that a little bit for the families who lost people in the crash. This win doesn't just go to us. It doesn't just go to the team and the coaches. It goes to the people who gave their lives for this team, something that they believed in and that they loved to do. There's no greater feeling now than to go out and feel the spirit outside that's surrounding Huntington right now."

I couldn't have said it better.

The players indeed showed that spirit. Michael Payton showed why he was the I-AA Player-of-the-Year and why he is the best player in America - poise and toughness. He made a lot of great throws. And he had more balls dropped than I can ever remember here. Troy demonstrated why he is a clutch guy and Hatch showed what he could do. This was the best team in Marshall history.

This championship was for Marshall.

chapter **14**▶

1993 SEASON

Football fans don't like the word "rebuilding" so I never mention it. Nevertheless, I looked at 1993 as just that. It was easy to see why when looking over the roster. We lost too many players from our championship team. Not just any players, but starters, and even more damaging, impact players. Payton was one. Troy Brown was another. So were Hatchett, Bartrum, and Andy Bowen. I was looking at a lot of lost offense alone. The offensive line had to be completely rebuilt. Phil Ratliff, Johnny McKee and Pete Woods left big holes. Defensively, we took a hit, too, although not as big as the offense. I had to replace four starters, Jim Durning, Byran Litton, Keenan Rhodes and Bob Lane, all linemen.

There was more depth on defense and I viewed the offense as one of major rebuilding. I couldn't hope to duplicate the firepower of the 1992 champions. They averaged 490 yards and 42 points a game to lead the country. That's a lot of thunder. Payton made most of the noise. I was going to miss him most of all. But I couldn't look back. I couldn't worry about the ones we lost because I had no control over that. I had to concern myself on who was coming back. That meant Todd. He had come full circle from only a year as a high school quarterback to two years as Payton's back-up. I looked back at my decision not to redshirt him for the 1991 season. If I had, I honestly felt that we wouldn't have won the championship. He filled in when Payton was hurt and won some big games to get us there.

In the two years Todd backed up Payton, he completed 92 of 165 passes for 1,340 yards, 15 touchdowns and only seven interceptions. Those were good enough numbers to build on. Two games in particular were fresh in my mind, one in his freshman year. Payton was ill and I had to start Todd cold against Western Carolina.

He led us to a playoff saving 27-24 triple overtime win. Then last year I saw him mature overnight. He replaced an injured Payton in the first quarter of a playoff game against Middle Tennessee State and stood tall. He completed 13 of 22 passes for 246 yards and three touchdowns in a big 35-21 win. The championship was ours after that.

Todd and I talked about that game when the season ended. He felt it was the best thing that had ever happened to him. Up until then, there was always some doubt in his mind. What was he going to do next season? Would he be able to do it after Payton left? He went into that playoff game and played well. That one game gave him the confidence he needed and the rationale for me to look to him to replace Payton for the 1993 season. It's strange, but Todd being here made me a better coach. I wasn't quite as hands-on with the players as I would have been if he wasn't here. I sit back now and watch a lot more of what's going on. I didn't get involved in just one particular phase. I was now trying to do a lot of everything.

Todd's emergence as a starter made it all worthwhile. Until then, I felt that perhaps I shouldn't have taken the Marshall job. It had been a bigger strain on my family than I had imagined. As much as I like Huntington, my team and everything about my job, I wouldn't do the family separation again. The time I got to spend with them my first year was just too limited. From a personal standpoint, I might not have taken the job. I'm glad I did, professionally. Todd was a major influence in my decision. He told me that I had to do it.

When I hesitated, he pushed me harder. He said, "Go. Mom and I will make the best of it." He knew how much I wanted to be a head coach. There were times when I remained in one place so I wouldn't have to move the family around. Todd told me that I had passed up too many opportunities, that I couldn't wait any longer and that he and his mother could handle it for a year. However, Todd had a lot more responsibilities. He had to watch out for his mother and make sure things were okay around the house. That had been my job and when it became Todd's, it put a damper on his senior year in high school. He was on his own, making decisions because I wasn't around. He grew up faster.

I never realized the void my first year in Huntington created in Norman. Todd mentioned that the hardest part of our separation was not being able to watch my team play. Since he was a little kid he had been involved with my coaching and knew what was going on. He didn't get to see any games in person but managed to watch two on satellite. It upset him because he wanted to be with me, especially after we beat Furman. It was my first big win as a head coach and Todd was upset because he and his mom weren't here to celebrate with me.

It was tough on Mary, too. She's meant so much to me over the years and I couldn't have gotten this far without her. She had been through a lot, being a coach's wife: the uncertainty, the relocating, trying to establish friendships while raising a family of three children. She confessed that the year's separation was a lot harder than she thought it would be. She understood that as a coach's wife one always went through adjustments. But, she claimed, this was the ultimate adjustment and hoped that she would never have to do it again. She hated the fact that she couldn't be here to experience it with me. As she put it, it was the first time that she'd missed an entire season.

The separation seemed like an eternity. We pulled together, though, and worked through it. I'm happy it worked out the way it did. We've always been a close family. Huntington is a sports town and the support is genuine. No matter who the coach is, the people would make him feel good. I had no idea of the magnitude until my dad died. The support astounded me. So many people I didn't even know made it a point to contact me. From a popularity standpoint, I knew I had some tough shoes to fill following George Chaump's departure. Yet, I was who I was and the people here accepted that and made me and my family feel welcome. Along the way you work hard and make sacrifices to reach the ultimate goal. And we did in 1992.

Looking back, I was glad that Earl Edwards had faith in me. I was close to him and I will never forget him. He was making changes. Several coaches on his staff were getting close to retirement age and I think he saw a bit of himself in me when he was my age. Edwards also recognized the fact that Bill Dooley at North Carolina and Paul Dietzel at South Carolina were the younger coaches in the Atlantic Coast Conference and were heavy recruiters. He felt that I could relate to younger players and would have a better chance recruiting against them. That was the start of it. Now, after 24 years, I feel a sense of satisfaction and accomplishment. I am happy I went the coach's route instead of the business world. I have enjoyed my success so far, 12 post-season appearances and two national championships.

Getting a third one in 1993 wasn't likely. I was anticipating winning six to seven games, nothing more. Everyone else in the Southern Conference was stronger and we were the new kid on the block they were pointing to. That's what comes with success. At the conference coaches' meeting that summer, the one we call the rouser, I was surprised that six of the nine coaches picked us to win the title. I thought Western Carolina and Georgia Southern looked stronger on paper. What do coaches know, anyway? I put us in a crap shoot with Appalachian State and Furman. But Marshall as conference favorites? I couldn't see that.

Lee Moon must have seen something, though. And I applaud him for the move he made. Months before our summer splash he changed the Western game, which was originally scheduled to be played in Cullowhee, to a home game in Huntington. I'll take any edge I can get and that was definitely an edge. Who knows how big that game could be at the end of the regular season, with the playoffs beginning the very next week? If we could win seven games and needed an eighth to make the playoffs, the outcome of the Western game could very well determine our chances.

I was determined to install an offense that best suited Todd's personality. His physical skills exceeded what was needed at quarterback and I started from there. The worst thing I could have done was expect him to do the same thing Payton did. He didn't have as strong an arm but was accurate, nonetheless. He wasn't as strong a runner as Payton but he was a little more elusive. However, he had more experience as a starter than Michael had when he first became a starter in 1990. Besides, Todd had been the only player since I've been coaching that I have bought a car for. Not many coaches can say that, unless they incur the wrath of the NCAA. But as I said, I'll take whatever edge I can get and I had a happy quarterback. We had grown closer the past two years.

I also had a potential star running back. Although Glenn Pedro was the incumbent and a senior, the more I studied film on Chris Parker the more I saw a big play runner. Almost lost in the euphoria of the championship 1992 season was what Parker accomplished as a sparingly used freshman. He ran for 620 yards, averaging 6.1 yards a carry. Those were Oklahoma numbers. He had a quick step which made him look faster than the 4.5 he ran in the forty. The other offensive weapons I had were wide receivers Will Brown and Ricky Carter. Carter, too, showed a great deal of ability as a freshman with 40 receptions that averaged 16.1 yards.

Still, the strength of the team was the defense keyed by linebackers Shannon King, William King and Donahue Stephenson, defensive end Rodney Garrett and defensive backs Roger Johnson and Shannon Morrison. It was the best defense to ever walk on a field for Marshall. We had more size than we had ever had. The defensive front was inexperienced but it would get better with each game. They would have to carry the ball and set up the offense. If the defense played tough, as I expected, then I was confident we could score enough points to win. We just had to stay focused.

It seemed that the opening game was always Morehead. It was no different this year. At practice during the week, Payton had a talk with Todd. He told him to relax and play his own game. Be your own quarterback and not me or any other quarterback that's played here, he told Todd. Tony Petersen, Marshall's quarterback in the 1987 championship game, mentioned the same thing, emphasizing to Todd that he had to play within himself and play within the offensive system which we installed.

We had a difficult two weeks of pre-season practice because of the excessive heat. I thought I was back at Florida State. I was a little concerned that we didn't progress as I expected, since there were injuries to some of the players, and that slowed our efforts. Morehead had installed a new set which opened up their offense. They were now multiple, running some options, but ready to throw the ball more.

It was a good feeling seeing 27,000 fans turn out for the opener. And the weather was even cooler, around 70 degrees, a far cry from the stifling heat weeks before. We started slow on offense and managed a 38-yard field goal by David Merrick near the end of the first period. Merrick did it again from the same distance midway through the second quarter. I was still uncomfortable until Melvin Cunningham ran a punt back 49 yards for our first touchdown. What really got me excited was our final series with 31 seconds left. Todd finally got on track. He took us 65 yards, completing all four passes he threw, the final one a 19 yarder to Brown that gave us a 21-0 halftime lead.

On Morehead's opening drive in the third period, Johnson recovered a fumble and ran it back 31 yards for a 28-0 advantage. Another Morehead fumble on their 44-yard line set up the next touchdown. Todd got it to Brown with a 20-yard pass and a 35-0 lead. That was more like it. When Parker scored from one yard out to finish a 51-yard drive in the opening minutes of the final period, I sent in Chad O'Shea to run the offense. He finished the game throwing only three passes, but two were for touchdowns. The first was 25 yards to Tim Martin and the other was 30 yards to Andre Womack for a 56-0 victory.

We generated 421 yards of offense, which was a good first effort. It was the defense that excelled, holding Morehead to 157 yards. It took the offense 29 minutes to score its first touchdown, but it didn't disturb me as much as it would have if Todd hadn't played well. He finished 18 of 26 for 224 yards and two touchdowns. And although it was only one game, I was pleased by our overall play. This was a relatively new unit on offense and I felt confident they would grow together.

I realized one thing - I had to get the ball more to Parker. He touched it only five times against Morehead. We ran 40 or 50 plays with the first team offense and 26 of them were passes and 13 were runs to Pedro. Parker should get the ball at least 15 times. He has the ability to hit a home run every time he touches it. We hadn't had that kind of back here before and he could be a big push for us throughout the year. You never knew when he would break one. I had to get him more involved. I explained about the lack of carries to Parker the week of the Murray State game and he understood, adding that he was patient.

Murray had dropped its home opener to Eastern Illinois, 34-17. Generally, a team makes improvements between the first and second games, or so I thought. That wasn't the case against Murray. Oh, we managed to win, 29-3, but it was far from pretty. Fact is, I called it ugly. But then a win is a win and what coach wouldn't take it. Only Parker looked pretty in that game.

State got on the board first with a 26-yard field goal. The offense again started slow and we had just begun to move when the first quarter ended. We completed a 77-yard drive in the opening minutes of the second period when Pedro ran around the right side for 12 yards and a 7-3 lead. Merrick booted a 35-yard field goal the next time we got the ball but, that was it. I wasn't at all pleased with a 10-3 half-time lead, even though Parker had run for 103 yards. What puzzled me was that the offensive line looked out of sync.

We still appeared sluggish in the third period. Still, we managed to score a touchdown when Pedro finished a 53-yard drive with a three yard run. I wasn't exactly jumping with joy with a 16-3 lead and another quarter to play. Merrick missing a field goal added to my frustration. What helped overcome it minutes later was Parker. He got outside and cruised for a 32-yard run into the end zone and I felt a little better at 22-3. When he did it again with a 20-yard dash, I was relieved with a 29-3 victory.

It certainly didn't come easy. It wasn't a performance I was proud of. We were flat except for Parker, who finished with 160 yards on 12 carries. Still, it was just that we were not near the offensive team I thought that we would be. At this point, I thought we'd be better. We didn't have any continuity on the offensive line. And Todd didn't have any, either. He played a bad first half but settled down after that. He tried to do too much and was pressing a bit, trying to make the big plays. He was looking downfield too much and wasn't taking what they were giving him. It wasn't anything that couldn't be corrected and I still felt that we could become a good team before it was over. We all had some growing to do.

Doubt is a strong emotion. It puts you in a distraught situation. I wanted the players to know that I had confidence in our potential. It's like being a parent. You just don't love your kids when they're right. This is the same deal. My approach was to tell the players that we were very fortunate not to lose a game when we didn't play very well, and that we've got to realize that things are going to be difficult every time we go out. We were going to get everybody's best shot.

We still hadn't gotten past the first chapter in our playbook, but we were getting close after Parker's breakthrough game against Murray. He had runs of 45, 32, 20, 15, 14 and 11 yards and demonstrated his ability to break tackles in the open field. I kept re-running the projector, watching him make one move after the other. That's something a coach can't teach. He would get even better and he was intent on becoming a complete player and not just one who depended only on speed. He learned from Hatchett about reading defenses but he wanted to establish his own identity. In his freshman year he had a problem catching the ball and the players kidded him about it. They called him "hands of stone" but he didn't look like Roberto Duran to me. He looked every bit a runner and his problem was not so much catching as it was relaxing.

Despite a 2-0 start and a No. 1 ranking, we couldn't relax. Not with Georgia Southern coming in. They, too, were 2-0 and ranked No. 7. It was our first conference game of the season and one in which we expected to be tested after two soft victories. I wasn't kidding myself. We really hadn't been challenged and this game would be an indicator of how we would do this season. I was playing it one game at a time and this was the first crossroads. Southern was big but we matched up with them. Their defense had given up only nine points and 424 yards in two games. This wasn't going to be one of those 40-point games. Rather, it was going to be a physical game with popping going on by both teams.

The players were looking forward to the challenge. They wanted to know just how good they really were. There was a lot of banter by the players all week that gave the game somewhat of a playoff atmosphere. I heard Rodney Garrett say that it may be the biggest regular season game he had ever played. Southern's double option offense was similar to a wing-T. However, they didn't pull as much with their guards which resulted in less faking. We stressed to the defense to play the run first. "Coach, I wish we could play teams like Southern every week!" exclaimed Shannon

King. I wasn't so sure yet.

Southern's reputation attracted over 29,000 fans. That's a playoff atmosphere and maybe King was right after all. I could feel the excitement in the stands. Melvin Cunningham gave us our first opportunity to score by recovering a fumble on Southern's 18-yard line with 2:30 remaining in the first period. Todd missed on two passes after Pedro got a yard and we had to be content with Merrick's 34-yard field goal. Midway through the period we scored what turned out to be the game's only touchdown. We drove 69 yards in eight plays with Todd and Will Brown collaborating on a 34-yard pass and a 10-0 lead. A 47-yard Southern field goal closed the first half scoring, 10-3. We had to keep playing defense. No one was going to light up the scoreboard.

On our opening drive in the third period we added another field goal. It was the longest Merrick ever made, 50 yards, which also set a stadium record, and it gave us a 13-3 lead. I had anticipated a low scoring game and it was. Those were the final points of the contest as neither team came close to scoring the rest of the game. I savored the victory. We hurdled our first barrier in a tough game. I tipped my cap to the players and told them that this was the first step in becoming a good football team. And I was becoming a big fan of defense. But I didn't lose sight of the fact that Parker carried the ball 25 times for 123 yards.

I never had a good feeling about playing Tennessee-Chattanooga, especially in Chattanooga. I don't know what it is, but we can't seem to beat them down there. Marshall was 1-7 in games played on Chamberlain Field. Maybe the stadium was the deterrent. Every time I think about the place I shudder. The 85-year-old edifice is a relic out of the past, embedded in a time capsule, like something out of a Stephen King movie. The players called the place ugly and I guess that's the best way to describe it. The fans seem more interested in annoying the other team than in watching the game itself.

Todd remembered the place. As a freshman he got his first start in Chattanooga when Payton couldn't play. Todd racked up the points but we still lost, 38-31. In fact, Chattanooga had won three of the last four games against us and hadn't lost to Marshall at home since 1987. It wasn't only me, it had to be that place. Other Marshall coaches before me must have experienced the same problems. Chattanooga held the series edge, 12-4.

In the four years that I've been at Marshall they had a running back, James Roberts, who could use our games as a personal highlight film. The year before I got here, he ran for 149 yards. In 1990, he ran for 127 yards and completed an option pass for a touchdown. The following year he ran for 117 yards. He didn't do anything against us in 1992 - only because he didn't play. Chattanooga also had a good quarterback in Kenyon Earl. He was 40 of 69 for 710 yards and six touchdowns in the four games Chattanooga split. Not only did he have a strong arm, but he was accurate and mobile, too. Playing on grass, and the fact that we've played poorer against Chattanooga than any other team in the conference, didn't leave me with good thoughts. And with the week off after the Georgia Southern game, I had longer to think about it.

I forgot everything bad after the first period. We scored twice to take a 14-0 lead and took the fans out of the game. Todd opened with an 80-yard drive that Parker capped with a two yard run. Near the end of the quarter, Parker did what I expected of him. He raced 71 yards for a touchdown and nobody laid a hand on him. We then matched field goals before Chattanooga got a touchdown with 48 seconds left on an eight yard pass from Earl that ended a 65-yard drive and got Chattanooga closer, 17-10.

I started to get that funny feeling when the third quarter started and Chattanooga tied the game. They did it on a big play, a 69-yard bomb from Earl to Terrell Owens. Five minutes later, Pedro got us back in front on a four yard run. I couldn't enjoy it. A minute later Earl dropped another touchdown bomb, this one for 53 yards to Owens. Tied 24-24 going into the final period, deja vu struck. Chattanooga took the lead for the first time on a field goal, 27-24. As the quarter wound down, I thought we had it won. Parker scored from a yard out to put us ahead 31-27 with five minutes left. We played pass but still couldn't stop Earl. He threw a game-winning 18-yard touchdown pass, to Owens of course, to pull the game out at the end, 33-31. It was 1991 all over again.

What happened to our defense? It was hard to believe they could annihilate us like that - 502 yards! We couldn't stop them at all. I thought we had really improved in the secondary but I was wrong. We busted so many coverages and left receivers wide open. It's no wonder that Earl didn't miss. He was 21 of 29 for 332 yards and four touchdowns, with all four caught by Owens. That's hard to beat. We should have been poised and confident down the stretch, but we weren't. There was no benefit from this game. Oh, yeah, Roberts got his 100 yards but Parker took the spotlight away from him. He had 209.

And I had some thinking to do. I tried to downplay the loss. I told the squad to forget it, that it wasn't the end of the world. I added that we were a good team with playoff potential. I found some solace in knowing we played VMI next. Six times Marshall has followed a loss with a beating of VMI and I viewed the game as a morale builder. They were winless in four games and what better elixir is there than that?

The VMI game was over by the first period. We scored 24 points and I could feel the team's confidence steadying. Brown started it with an 11-yard touchdown pass from Todd. By halftime it was 38-0. I kept Todd in longer to restore his confidence and he responded with 23 of 33 for 258 yards in the 51-0 rout on a windy, wet night. Todd had been feeling some pressure because the offense hadn't played well the first three games of the season and he heard it from the critics when he didn't pull out the Tennessee-Chattanooga game.

This hasn't been something out of Grimm's Fairy Tales for Todd. And playing North Carolina State just added to the story line. I had played there, and now Todd would follow in my footsteps on the same field in Carter-Finley Stadium. If you ask me about playing against my alma mater, I would say honestly I'd rather not. We have no business playing a I-A school. We're physically outmatched even before taking the field. I-A schools have 85 scholarships while I-AA has only 65. Go figure. The kids love the challenge to show that they can play at that level. But the stark reality of the whole situation is picking up $100,000 in a David and Goliath match-up, which is not my idea of what this program is all about.

State was 3-2 but they played in the Gator Bowl last season, one of five bowl appearances the last five years. I mean, what am I doing here? This wasn't some Willie-off-the-pickle boat-team. And we couldn't sneak up on them as we did two years ago. In 1991 we had them beat 14-3 with a minute left to play until they scored twice to beat us, 15-14. What a heartbreaker that was. I didn't want any more of those. Yet the over-riding issue that stuck in my mind, and will forever, is how poorly we played offensively. The game was lost simply because we hit only 10 of 30 passes for the entire contest. We had plenty of chances and should have won.

I didn't like the start this time. Todd got sacked for 14 yards on the six yard line the very first play of the game. Yet, we kept our composure after Parker got outside for 23 yards on the very next play. That gave us a big lift and we continued on an 80-yard march for a touchdown, Parker going over from seven yards out. The next time we had the ball we went 62 yards with Todd hitting Carter in the right corner of the end zone with an eight yard pass. Just like that it's 14-0 and I wondered if Earle Edwards was watching.

When we opened the second quarter with Merrick's 27-yard field goal, I was beginning to think that this might be David's day against Goliath. The kick gave us a 17-7 lead at half-time. The one thing that concerned me was that State drove 96 yards, which can wear down a defense in the second half, just before Merrick booted his field goal. We had played State even and Parker showed that he could play on the I-A level by gaining 125 yards.

State added a field goal, which took care of the scoring in the third period. We had 15 minutes left in the game and like the last time we were ahead, 17-10. How many times has it been said that games are won or lost in the fourth quarter? Well, this was another. State tied the game with another long drive, 81 yards. There was more. The next time they drove 85 yards for the winning touchdown with two minutes left. It was 1992 all over again. Only the score was different, 24-17. The kids played their hearts out, a heart-wrenching, gut-wretching game. I didn't want to look at the films. Ever.

The only satisfaction I got out of the North Carolina State loss was that we put some good drives together which didn't leave us hanging our heads for Appalachian State. They were another nemesis. They had beaten us two straight times, which knocked us out of the conference championship. At 1-6, they didn't appear to be an attractive opponent for Homecoming Day. It was their worst start in 14 years but there was a reason for it. No one can win many games committing 19 turnovers and having six punts blocked. Breaking them down further, they had given the ball to the other team 27 times on the other side of the 40-yard line. Yet, the only loss we incurred in 24 home games was to Appy last year, 37-34. I didn't want a repeat of that disappointment.

Todd had the scoreboard operator busy, first with a 25-yard pass to Martin that culminated an 80-yard drive. After Appy opened the second quarter with a field goal, the offense caught fire and scored three touchdowns. Brown got the first one on a 25-yard pass from Todd. Pedro accounted for the next one with a six-yard run. Then, in the closing minutes of the half, Todd found Brown again, this time with a seven-yard pass. At the break we were in control, 28-3.

Two minutes before the third quarter ended, we scored the last points of the game. Parker swept in from the nine yard line to give us a convincing 35-3 triumph. I couldn't say enough about the defense, which allowed only 233 yards. In 20 quarters at home they hadn't allowed a touchdown. Our offense had 490 yards and I felt that Todd had his best game of the year, 14 of 21 passes for 199 yards and three touchdowns that must have convinced some others, too, in the crowd of 25,000.

On the way down to Charleston, South Carolina, I did some heavy thinking. Before the season began, I was convinced that it was going to be a rebuilding one with the following year being our year. Now, I wasn't so sure. Maybe we could sneak up this year. Wouldn't that be great? At 5-2 I felt we could control our own destiny. We weren't as good as last year, but if we could make the playoffs and play some games at home, anything could happen.

The offensive philosophy that we re-designed before the season started to kick in. In the last two years, we had used the pass to set up the run. Now it was the opposite. We used the run to set up the pass because Todd didn't have the arm strength of Payton or the big play receivers. Parker played a big part in our thinking. The opponents were looking at him first rather than keying on Todd. That was a big advantage for a young offense. And we were still that after seven games.

The Citadel was 3-5 but they had that wishbone that I left back in Oklahoma. Funny, but nobody in town had shown any trepidation about my installing it at Marshall. It had taken them that long to forget about it. Winning does that. And Todd started us in that direction with two quick first period touchdowns the first two times we had possession. He directed a 64-yard drive by getting Parker in on a three yard pitch out. Then he led us 81 yards with the touchdown coming on a four yard pass to Carter.

In the second period we scored twice again. The first drive covered 83 yards. Parker made it happen with another pitch out that went for 28 yards. After Citadel scored, we padded our half-time margin to 28-7 with 15 seconds left. This time we went 74 yards with Todd hitting Parker with a quick three yard pass. I couldn't find any fault with the way the offense played. Todd was 13 of 14 with two touchdowns and Parker already had 92 yards.

After a scoreless third quarter, we clinched it in the early minutes of the fourth. On the same pitch out, Parker scored his fourth touchdown from the 28-yard line and we won 35-15. Todd set a Marshall single game accuracy record with his 17 of 20 completions. And for the second straight game he wasn't intercepted. I complimented Parker on another 100-yard game.

"Coach, that was a record for me," he exclaimed.

"It is?"

"Yeah. This was the first college game I ever played in the rain."

We had three more games to play, two of them at home. Furman was the away game in between East Tennessee State and the season closer against Western Carolina. There wasn't much to the mathematics. If we could win two of the three games, I figured we would make the playoffs with an 8-3 record, the same as the year before. I derived a great deal of satisfaction at the prospect because down in my heart I really didn't expect it.

There were now a lot of people comparing this team to the 1992 one. Not so. The comparison I made is that this team was developing like the team in 1991, getting better as the season progressed. Nobody, including myself, had any way of knowing how good we were going to be. The year I put down as the big one was 1994 when we would have so many returnees and at that point everybody would pick us to win it all. Our offense was feeding off the defense. We realized that if we didn't turn the ball over, we would have a good shot at winning the close games. The defense acquired a lot more confidence knowing that our offense could score some points. Parker needed only 38 yards to reach 1,000 and Todd completed 71 of his last 98 passes in making the offense click.

After East Tennessee converted a field goal, we went 70 yards in only six plays to take a 7-3 lead on Parker's eight-yard run. Two field goals by Merrick left it at 13-3 when the first period ended. We got some special teams help as the second quarter was coming to a close. Martin ran a punt back 47 yards just the way Troy Brown used to do. Merrick then added another field goal and we went into the dressing room with a 23-3 lead. Amazingly, we had the ball just over eight minutes and scored 23 points.

East Tennessee scored its only touchdown just after the fourth quarter began. That was it for them. We got another field goal from Merrick, and Erik Thomas closed out the scoring with a one yard plunge for a 33-9 triumph. We had one of the two wins. Yet, I wasn't all together pleased. We weren't as impressive as Parker, who ran for 202 yards. Maybe the players were looking ahead to Furman.

I wasn't exactly looking forward to going to Greenville on Homecoming Day. With our No. 2 ranking we were a target. Furman, despite being 4-4, was probably the best team we played in a month. When we took over here, we felt that Furman was the team we had to beat to get where we wanted to be in the league. We'd moved up and strangely they'd moved down a little bit. It was hard to believe that over the last 26 games we were 20-6 and they were 12-13-1. We had beaten them three straight years but this game was huge for our program. Winning would ensure that we'd be in the playoffs. If we lost, then we'd have to beat Western Carolina and hope to get in. That in itself made this a much bigger game.

Furman wasn't a pleasant place to play, not after losing seven of eight games there. By the end of the day it was eight of nine. Furman's defense looked like the Dallas Cowboys. We didn't come close to scoring a touchdown and they smothered us, 17-3. I knew after the first half that we would be in for a long day. Furman was ahead 3-0 at the time, but our offense wasn't making the plays we needed. The two times we had a chance to score, we failed when Merrick's kicks went awry. We had the ball twice as long as Furman and couldn't score. It was an omen.

It took us until the final five minutes of the third quarter to finally get on the board. Merrick booted a 24-yard field goal and we went into the fourth quarter tied, 3-3. It didn't stay that way long. Furman drove 68 yards for one touchdown and then came back 65 yards for the other. I was devastated. The loss not only diminished our playoff chances but also all hopes of winning the conference title. That hurt most of all. Marshall had never been Southern Conference champions.

I was at a loss for words and couldn't say anything. I felt bad for the kids. It was the first time offensively all year that we didn't have the spark we needed to win the game. Seven times we got into Furman's territory and couldn't get a touchdown. One touchdown would have changed the outcome. We'd had a problem getting the ball into the end zone the last two weeks. I couldn't explain it. I had to come up with some answers quickly before the Western Carolina game. We were now fighting for our lives to make the playoffs.

Before the season began, this game was looked upon potentially as the one that would determine the conference championship. Western was picked as the I-AA's best team in a number of pre-season polls. They were 6-4 but were a hot team after winning five of their last six games. A four-point loss to Appalachian State the previous week snapped their winning streak. In hindsight, I felt Western wished that they hadn't sold the game back to us in the spring.

I wasn't completely sold on our offense. The first unit hadn't scored a touchdown in seven quarters. Instead of peaking, it was slumping and it baffled me. Maybe I was depending too much on Parker. Perhaps I was better off opening up the offense more. Or it could have been that Parker was tired. I decided to talk to him about it. He assured me that he was fine and felt fresh. Yet, I was convinced that we were looking to him too much and would be better off mixing it up against Western.

We opened up by passing more and wound up with a field goal after we had reached Western's 20-yard line. Western then went ahead on a long drive. They went 86 yards in 15 plays that seemed like a lifetime. But we came back with a drive of our own that began on the 26 and took just as long. Unfortunately, we weren't successful. We reached Western's four yard line ready to take back the lead. On third down Todd's pass was intercepted by Julius Grant and run back 99 yards for a touchdown that pushed Western on top, 13-3. What a shocker. A play like that could kill a team. We had to bounce back before the half and did. With five minutes remaining, we went 79 yards with Parker getting the final three. The touchdown got us back in the game, 13-10, but just as important, it helped us psychologically. Just like last week, we had the ball twice as long and still were behind.

The season all came down to 30 minutes. We finally took the lead in the third period on a drive that was one of the biggest all year. It was a pressure drive because we started on the nine yard line and drove the length of the field. Todd made two big plays, the first a 41-yard pass to Martin and the other a 34-yard throw to Casey Hill that resulted in the touchdown that put us in front, 17-13. However, Western got closer with a field goal when the period concluded, 17-16. The season was reduced to one point and 15 minutes.

After Western missed a 36-yard field goal, it was our turn. We got as far as Western's 15 before being stopped. Merrick's 36-yard field goal gave us a little more breathing room, 20-16, with 5:34 left in the game and the regular season. The defense took over at that point and stopped Western the two times they had the ball. We finished 8-3 and, hopefully, with a berth in the playoffs. Yet, I didn't enjoy the victory. I heard the boos from the Marshall crowd during the game and couldn't believe my ears. I was still upset after I showered to go home. I didn't want to talk to anybody. Mary tried to help by telling me to forget it, but I couldn't.

chapter 15 ►

1993
PLAYOFFS

I reflected about the booing the next day after I found out that Howard University was our first round opponent in the playoffs. Boos are a part of the game but I felt a lot of them were directed at me because Todd is my son. I thought in the first half against Western, except for perhaps three plays, Todd had one of the best halves he had all year. I realized that the 99-yard interception incensed the crowd, but it could happen to anybody. But in this case that anybody was Todd. The defensive back made a great reaction to the ball and made a bang-bang play that upset the fans. The important thing was that it didn't upset the players and the bottom line was that we won. I had a talk with Todd about it the night before, just after dinner.

"Son, don't let the booing get you down."

"I'm fine, Dad."

"We've got the playoffs coming up this week and you have to put these things behind you."

"I already have. The booing is nothing new. The fans have given me a hard time all year. That's their prerogative, I guess. Hey, it comes with the territory."

"That's the way to look at it. But what counted was the way you bounced back after that, overcoming the adversity."

"I knew I had the support of my teammates. They gave me the strength to go out in the second half and do what I had to do to win the game. They carried me a long way."

"Well then, take it from there."

I thought Todd showed a lot of maturity in the way he addressed the situation.

Still, I didn't like the distraction at all. It was the same way I felt when Michael Payton was booed. I guess it's a sign of the times. But that doesn't mean I have to accept it. I was mad about the way it happened. It disgusted me. We've had a home field advantage for practically all our games, but I didn't particularly feel that comfortable now. I know our players didn't like it and I certainly didn't want to begin the playoffs on a downer.

The booing affected Mary, too. They weren't booing No. 15, they were booing her son. She had to sit out there in the stands listening to all of it, and unable to do anything about it. The fans may forget about it the next day but the memory will remain with Mary. Todd or anybody else shouldn't be subjected to boos. They're just kids, not pros. The players had worked so hard to reach the playoffs and now this had to happen.

I didn't get much time to study Howard. We didn't see them play all season and never had them scouted. All I had to go on was the films we exchanged with them. They had what I called a sic-'em defense. They came after you on every snap, took a lot of chances and pressured you. That left me thinking - we had the potential to make some big plays against them if we could break the line of scrimmage. Offensively, they reminded me of our 1992 team. They could run the ball when they needed to, had a couple of big play receivers and a quarterback who was mobile enough to move around, which made him difficult to sack. They played wide open, underneath routes, crossing patterns, screens and even going deep. And putting four wide-outs to one side was something we hadn't seen before. We decided to go with the run to offset their rush.

The first play we designed was a surprise that we had put in on Monday - a reverse. Erik Thomas made it look as though he ran it all his life. He broke it for 60 yards and a touchdown. Casey Hill gave us another scoring opportunity minutes later by recovering a fumble on Howard's 26-yard line. Parker got nine, then nothing, and came back for 17 and a touchdown. Run, run, run and we were up 14-0 before Howard knew what hit them. I was glad about our fast start.

Midway in the second period Howard tied the game. The quick start was suddenly equalized. We had to score on our next possession to stop the momentum and we did. Staying on the ground, we went 54 yards with Parker going in from the goal line for a 21-14 half-time lead. Howard had gained 100 more yards than us but I felt our defense played well. I told the offense that we were getting the second half kickoff and I wanted a touchdown. Todd had injured his thumb in the first quarter and I didn't know how long he could go. I knew he couldn't throw much.

It happened. We went 66 yards in seven plays and went up 28-14. Todd got us the touchdown with a 30-yard pass to Carter. I never imagined that the touchdown would be the last points of the game. And I couldn't believe how supportive the crowd was. Cold and rain kept it to less than 14,000, but I never heard a single boo.

I was glad that Delaware beat Montana. If they hadn't, then we would have gone to Montana for the quarter-final game. I didn't want that. It wasn't that I disliked the state. Montana is pretty country but not when its so cold in the winter. Delaware played an outstanding game to come from behind and beat second seeded Montana 49-48 in frigid conditions. That type of weather isn't for me. Besides, Montana was a long way to go to play a football game. We would have lost a day of practice and a long trip at this time of the season, after having played 12 games, could take its toll on the players.

Coach Tubby Raymond had been using a tricky wing-T at Delaware for as long as I could remember. He was the last of the dinosaurs and I don't think he liked us. We didn't know what to expect when we beat him last year in the quarter-finals. But now we did. He went with the same game plan. We gave our scout team a lot of work at practice all week preparing for their intricate offense. Their defense was their Achilles heel. They gave up an average of 28 points and 421 yards a game and all I could hope for was that our offense was healthy enough to take advantage.

Todd's thumb was swollen but our trainer, Jaime Perez, was convinced that it would be gone by game time. He wasn't sure about some of the others. Parker had sprained his knee and all we allowed him to do was run straight ahead during the workouts. Ricky Carter's knee was slowing him down and Tim Martin was struggling with a broken toe. Other than that, we were healthy. Hah! I had four key players on offense hurting and I had to go for the Tylenol.

Another rainy Saturday kept the crowd to less than 14,000. That says something for dome stadiums. I didn't need any more headache pills because all players dressed. Only Martin wouldn't be available for full-time duty and we would spot him according to the situation. If Parker's knee didn't hold up, then Pedro would step in and do most of the running. Todd assured me he could grip the ball without difficulty. I could see by the players' moods that they were eager to attack Delaware's defense. They showed it, too, after the kickoff. They went 80 yards in only five plays and Todd's 58-yard bomb to Casey Hill dispelled any fears about his thumb. Wow, 58 yards to a tight end. That had to be a Marshall record. Parker's three-yard run gave us a 7-0 lead and I couldn't feel the rain.

However, Delaware answered with a 68-yard drive that tied it. They added three more on a field goal for a 10-7 edge when the period ended. We got the ball back halfway through the second quarter. Martin, broken toe and all, positioned the touchdown with a 42-yard punt return to Delaware's 31 yard line. Minutes later, Parker took it in from the five to make it 14-10. Yet, once more Delaware retaliated. They went 63 yards to assume a 17-14 half-time advantage.

I didn't want to get into a high scoring game with Delaware, but it was heading that way. We had to get more offense in the second half to control the ball more. We started with an 80-yard drive which Parker completed with a three-yard run for his third touchdown. Merrick later added a 26 yard field goal and when the period ended, we were up 24-17. When Parker got his fourth touchdown opening the fourth period, I thought we finally shook Delaware. We had scored 17 straight points to push our edge to 31-17. But Delaware didn't quit. They went 73 yards on a drive for one touchdown and 65 for another, and with 1:14 left, it was 31-31.

I was thinking about overtime until Martin ran the kickoff back 39 yards to Delaware's 37. I feel fortunate that they didn't squib the kick. My heart skipped a beat when Martin fumbled until Brian Stump came out of nowhere to make the recovery. All we needed was field goal position and I wanted Parker to get us there. We had all three time-outs remaining so the clock was not a serious factor in going with the run. He got five, then eight and a timeout at 0:22. Then two more and another time out at 0:16. Time for one more run and Parker got a yard up the middle and a final time out at 0:07. Merrick time. Delaware called a time out to rattle him. He was unfazed. He kicked a 38-yard game winner that put us in the semi-finals, 34-31. I didn't know how much more excitement I could take.

Stump had provided the most excitement. There were three or four Delaware players around when he came up with the fumble. They actually had the ball covered, but Stump just reached in and took it out of the pile. It said a lot about the character of this team. Everybody wanted to contribute. That was a major factor in the win. So was Parker's effort, 144 yards and four touchdowns. I didn't miss Todd's three scrambles either. He turned potential sacks into meaningful yardage that led to three touchdowns.

I didn't know much about Troy State or McNeese State except that we would play the winner in the semi-finals. What I did know was that if Troy won, we would be home again. Guess who I was rooting for? The other semi was Georgia Southern at Youngstown State, which got my mind racing. I was pulling for Troy to win so we could play at home and I was hoping that Southern could do the same, which would be good for the Southern Conference.

After spending hours in the dark watching films of Troy State, I was convinced they were the best team we would play in the playoffs. Howard was a passing team and Delaware was a running team but Troy was something else. They could do both well. I was impressed with their quarterback, Kelvin Williams, who was a transfer from Alabama. I wished he had stayed there. He completed 178 of 281 passes for 2,752 yards and 29 touchdowns and amazingly only six interceptions. Maybe he snuck in from the NFL. They also had three 500-yard runners and a receiver, Orlando Parker, who had been a starter at Auburn. Was I missing something? How did all these big time players wind up at Troy? What Troy did was basically run two different offenses, a power set with the traditional I-plays and a four wide receiver set out of the shotgun.

Cold, wintry weather resulted in a small crowd of just over 14,000. Our defense got us going. Chris Hamilton recovered a fumble on Troy's 27-yard line. Five plays later, Parker scored from the two. Merrick then got into the act with a 37-yard field goal. Special teams contributed to the next touchdown. Albert Barber blocked a punt that LeRon Chapman scooped up on the five and ran in for a touchdown. I never expected a 17-0 lead when the second period began. I could only hope it would last. It didn't. Troy, with Williams throwing, came back. He started it with a 16-yard touchdown pass. Then we helped them. A bad snap from center prevented Colquitt from punting, which set Troy up on our 26. They scored in five plays and suddenly it was 17-14. However, we kept our poise and drove 79 yards and Todd got it done. He hit Martin with a 17-yard touchdown pass and a 24-14 lead. Still, we couldn't shake Troy. They scored with a minute to go on Williams' three-yard pass. We barely held on, 24-21.

I never expected it to end that way. I was looking at an 80-point game. But both team's defenses took over in the second half and neither offense threatened to score. Not even a field goal. Football can be a strange game. I had hoped to keep the ball away from Troy, but I never thought the second half would result in a shutout for both teams. We owned the clock for 19 minutes and kept giving the ball to Parker. He finished with 31 carries and 129 yards, another fine effort. I also took the harness off Todd and told him he could run if he had an opening. That made him smile because he likes to run. After the game, Todd gave me a hug in the middle of the field and I hoped everyone saw it. This was a bonding between father and a son that went beyond coach and player. He whispered something special, "I love you, Dad," and I'll never forget that moment.

chapter 16

1993
CHAMPIONSHIP

It was Youngstown again! I don't know if anyone in Hollywood could have dreamed up this script. For the third straight year we met Youngstown in the NCAA Division I-AA championship game. *USA Today's* Danny Sheridan said the odds on that happening were a million to one. The rivalry had reached a crescendo. It was the rubber match in the series and CBS had a story line they could work the whole game. Youngstown came from behind in the final quarter to beat us 25-17 in 1991 and Willy Merrick came off the bench to kick a last second field goal in our 31-28 victory in 1992. I don't know how there could be any more drama. They had their storybook ending and so did we, but it was time to put the fairy tales aside.

Todd and I had a good talk at dinner. He was looking forward to playing Youngstown. The entire team was, for that matter. There were 14 seniors still around from the 1991 game and they wanted to leave with another ring. Todd especially wanted one because the way he looked at it he didn't contribute much last year.

"Dad, I'm fired up for this one. I played only a small part in it last time."

"Well, your role is different this year."

"That's true. I feel a big part of this championship team."

"I've watched you grow out there and I feel you're capable of getting it done. You've overcome a lot of criticism."

"I think the way that I have played in the playoffs and the way the team has rallied around me really showed that I didn't care what people were saying about me."

"You've demonstrated that. The entire team has accomplished more than was expected of them. We were supposed to be rebuilding this year."

"I'm just going to go on playing as hard as I can, and whatever happens in this last game, I'm going to be satisfied."

"It's been a difficult season for both of us. You've handled it better than I did."

"Hey, I'm glad you finally decided to let me run with the ball more. You know how much I like to do that and it's helped in getting us some first downs."

"I couldn't chance getting you hurt by running. We didn't have anybody behind you."

"But it's nice having another option rather than staying back there and taking a beating. I love running with the ball."

"Just remember, you're no Chris Parker."

Parker had a phenomenal year. Before the season, he had set a personal goal of 1,000 yards but didn't think it was a great challenge, so he increased it to 1,500. He exceeded it with 1,703 yards and 24 touchdowns. I was worried that he might have been a little tired for the playoffs, but he kept right on running. In the three playoff games he ran for 333 yards and seven touchdowns. We felt that Parker was the dominant offensive player in the conference. When considering that everybody keyed on him and he was still able to be so productive said a lot for his ability.

I thought about what Chris Deaton went through and it symbolized the success we had had this year. We truly never expected him to play football ever again. He came off major surgery in February that left him with two metal plates in his head. He had been out late one night, three o'clock in the morning, and was hungry, which wasn't unusual for a 275 pound tackle. The only place open that late at night was Taco Bell on the east end of town. He was alone when he pulled up to the drive-through window. Out of nowhere, he was assaulted by three teenagers. One of them had a bat and another had a beer bottle, which they used on Deaton's head.

It was a wonder that he was alive. For months he could only move his head to one side. Needless to say, he missed spring practice but came by every day and attended the meetings. I felt very bad for him. "Don't count me out, Coach," he always told me. He made it back and never missed a game the entire four years he played, even overcoming a concussion in the Tennessee-Chattanooga game. What a display of courage! It rubbed off on the rest of the team. Like Joe DiMaggio, Deaton finished with a streak of 56 consecutive games that may never be broken. And my players were finished with Taco Bell. I told them if they were craving Mexican food to ring Jaime Perez's doorbell instead and he'd make them some tacos.

Before the Troy State game I decide to use psychology on the players. On Friday evening when the players were at the movies, I had Scott Reese tape the names of the Troy players above each individual's locker. When they returned to the locker room and saw what happened, they went into a rage. "No way is Troy going to use our lockers," they yelled. If Troy had beaten us, they were designated as the home team for the championship game. I didn't have to use any such motivation for Youngstown. The rivalry was hot enough.

Any team that reached the championship game was good. And Youngstown was that. They weren't given much notice in the pre-season polls, which only showed how wrong polls can be at times. Youngstown was a huge team, pro size all the way, and the biggest team we faced all year with an offensive line that averaged 298 pounds. I hoped to offset their size with quickness. Their coach, Jim Tressel, was becoming an old friend. Three times in three years we played each other for the championship. We knew what each other would do and he liked to control the ball on the ground. And why not? He had two 1,000-yard runners that he depended on. Tamron Smith with 1,344 yards and Darnell Clark with 1,124 were both strong runners.

This was our 12th playoff game in three years and I was tremendously proud of what we had accomplished. For me, it was my sixth national championship game in nine years, but I was a little edgy for this one. Our practice sessions during the week were disrupted by final exams. It wasn't fair for the players to practice under that strain. It's difficult to do both. I just hoped the expected crowd of 30,000 would give us an edge. We had won 29 of 30 games at home and I wanted just one more.

I depended on the defense, which was our strength all season, to make the difference. They excelled at stopping the run. If we won the coin toss, I planned on deferring, which meant we would kick off. There were two good reasons for my strategy. I wanted to pin Youngstown deep on the kickoff, get a turnover and a quick score. Being behind early, Youngstown couldn't control the ball with the run. Secondly, by getting the second half kickoff, we would be able to control the ball with Parker. This was the best approach to a second straight championship.

The worst possible scenario happened. Instead of kicking deep, Merrick's kickoff sailed out of bounds. I looked away in disgust. There wasn't any negative field position to force a turnover. Rather, Youngstown comfortably had the ball on the 35-yard line. One errant kick destroyed the strategy. It also took the edge off the defense. Smith busted up the middle for 15 yards to midfield. Then Clark left us stunned by bolting 50 yards for a touchdown. Bang, bang, two plays and it was 7-0. The quick touchdown fired up Youngstown's defense. We couldn't advance the ball from the 20 and had to punt. Another faux pas. The snap went over Colquitt's head and he was downed on the five-yard line. Smith scored two minutes later and it was 14-0 before anybody could even finish a hot dog. This wasn't supposed to happen. Everything we had carefully planned was negated. We now had to play catch-up football. I bit my lip in anger. This was not what I wanted.

We made only one first down before we had to punt a second time. Then Youngstown really turned on the pressure. They went on a 15-play drive that lasted seven minutes. On third and four on the five, we stopped them from scoring another touchdown. They kicked a field goal instead for a 17-0 lead. What killed us on that drive was the fact that their quarterback, Mark Brungard, who wasn't a passing threat all season, completed two big third down throws. Our offense stalled for the third time as the period ended. Youngstown dominated the first 15 minutes with eight first downs to our one. I don't ever remember playing such an inept first quarter.

The second period was no better. Yet, we had a chance to break through in the beginning and blew it. William King recovered a fumble on the Youngstown 24, just the way I pictured it when we kicked off to start the game. But after Parker gained two yards, he fumbled on the next play. I wanted to hide. We needed some points at that point but never threatened. The rest of the period the offense had trouble moving the ball and got past midfield only once. Youngstown had one more shot at a field goal, but Danny White blocked it at the 42. It was an ugly first half. We had three first downs and 42 net yards. Total embarrassment.

The Youngstown defense was taking away the middle, so we put in some outside routes at half-time in an attempt to spread them. If we could do something, move the ball, kick a field goal or even a touchdown with the second half kickoff, we'd get back into the game with a momentum swing. The offense managed to shake off some of its inertia by going 45 yards before bogging down on the Youngstown 35. We almost had a touchdown during the drive but Carter dropped Todd's 38-yard pass in the end zone. Maybe the drive was a sign that the offense was coming out of its lethargy. I could only hope so. When we got the ball again, we looked snappy. Todd completed all three of his passes and we went from the 20 to Youngstown's 18-yard line. A touchdown would turn the game around. However, Parker could get only eight yards on three carries and we had to be content with Merrick's 27-yard field goal. Hopefully, the 70-yard drive was a spark. There was one more quarter left to find out.

Youngstown kept the pressure on. They reached our 17-yard line in the early moments of the fourth quarter before being stopped. Their 34-yard field goal attempt was wide. We had to score a touchdown and I don't recall ever coming closer and not doing it. Starting on the 20, we put together our best drive of the day. Todd hit five of six passes and also had a 13-yard run to take us to the Youngstown three-yard line. We needed the six now. Parker lost a yard, then gained two to the two-yard line. Todd got one more. On fourth and one it was Parker's turn again. He had done it all year. This was his game. He went up top but was stopped in mid-air. At first I thought the ball was over the goal line. But he carried it low and didn't extend his arm, and the official didn't give him the touchdown. With five minutes left, the crowd was quiet.

It didn't matter that Youngstown took a safety. At 17-5, we still needed two touchdowns. We tried to get one but Todd's desperation pass was intercepted on the Youngstown seven-yard line. Youngstown ran out the final 1:40 and there was no last minute drama this time. Our defense had done a tremendous job after the first period, but our offense never broke out. I never imagined that we would never score a touchdown. Not one. Our season was over at 11-4 but there wasn't any championship. I had an empty feeling.

Youngstown flat outplayed us. It just wasn't meant to be, I guess. They got off to a great start and we couldn't establish our running game. When was the last time Parker gained only 47 yards and lost a fumble? Probably in grade school. Remember my belief about three plays determining the outcome of a close game? Well, there they were: Colquitt not getting his punt off in the first quarter; Carter dropping a touchdown pass in the third quarter; and Parker not getting in for a touchdown in the fourth quarter.

We had to seize the moment, but didn't. Still, if there was any solace, I felt good about our future. We'll be back.